work

work
to
me

GROSSET
GOOD LIFE
BOOKS

Home Remodeling

Home Remodeling

BY A.J. HARMON, A.I.A.

GROSSET
GOOD LIFE
BOOKS

PUBLISHERS • GROSSET & DUNLAP • NEW YORK

Text and illustrations by A. J. Harmon
Cover photograph by Mort Engel

Copyright © 1975 by A. J. Harmon
All rights reserved
Published simultaneously in Canada
Library of Congress catalog card number: 74-33764
ISBN 0-448-12002-X (trade edition)
ISBN 0-448-13311-3 (library edition)
First printing
Printed in the United States of America

Some of the illustrative material in this book previously appeared in *The Guide to Home Remodeling* by A. J. Harmon, copyright © 1966 by A. J. Harmon, and is reproduced here by permission of Holt, Rinehart and Winston, Inc.

Contents

1
The Importance
of Remodeling

The United States is the first nation in history in which every citizen can—and many expect to—own his own home. If you are reading this introductory page of a book devoted completely to remodeling, you probably already own a house or are thinking of buying one and remodeling it to suit your needs. We do outgrow our homes and the way you live now may have changed markedly from the way you lived at the time you bought your house.

Perhaps your children have grown so that the small bedrooms are no longer adequate for sharing. They need separate spaces to enjoy hobbies and entertain their friends. Teen-agers especially need a quiet place to think and study away from youngsters whose bedtimes are much earlier than their own. You as a parent may need a study or a den to get away from the noisier activities of children's games and television programs to pursue your own hobbies and interests.

You may find that some rooms are not used as they were planned to be, while others are used constantly, and a redesigning and remodeling of the existing interior space will gain you more useful rooms without the expense of an addition. It is possible that you may need to add a separate apartment for an elderly member of the family, or turn a little used playroom into a nursery. As the size of your family grows and teen-agers take a more active interest in cooking, you will find the kitchen too small and inconvenient for those who want to learn and the once efficient counter space crowded with helping hands.

The problem of undersized and overutilized bathrooms is practically universal, whether it is the morning rush hour or soiled towels and steamy walls just before dinner guests arrive. Or it could be that all you really want is your own bathroom off the master bedroom so that you can shower and shave without picking your way through your daughter's curlers and panty-hose. A second or third bathroom addition can be a luxurious extravagance, but only under unusual conditions, such as the house needs a new roof instead. The cost of a well-designed practical bathroom addition can be less than the cost of moving two blocks down the street and will increase the value and salability of your property.

Our lives and the way we live change constantly. Our houses should not

Identical when built and occupied (top), *houses come to reflect the character of the owners* (bottom).

only reflect that change, but accommodate it and make the change easier. The best way to get the most comfort, use, and enjoyment out of your house is to remodel it to suit the changes. Of course, there are alternatives to remodeling the house you live in. You can buy another house to remodel or you can build or buy a new house.

Buying a house to remodel, because of the cost of refinancing, changing interest rates, and moving, is almost always more expensive than remodeling the house you already own. You should also be aware of the fact that another house will not be without its unexpected pitfalls, not only those inherent in the structural and mechanical aspects, but in those eccentricities that exist in every house. An unfamiliar garden, neighborhood, and perhaps a different school for the children can be problems. With your own house, you already have a good idea of what is wrong with it and what it needs to put it in tip-top condition.

Building or buying a new house in the suburbs may solve some families' problems, but too often it creates serious new ones for both the family and the community. In the past, too many people sold their homes in the middle of town when they outgrew them and joined the exodus to the suburbs. They left behind an area in which there were schools, hospitals, fire and police protection, public utilities, and transportation, creating a need for these services to be duplicated elsewhere, and leaving the heart of the towns and cities to decay. Families moving into newly built tract houses have been confronted with fireplaces that billow smoke and streak freshly painted walls, rusty tap water that turns bathtubs and sinks brown, furnaces that overheat kitchens but do not warm bathrooms, windows that will not open, and garages and basements that flood when it rains. So it should come as no surprise that my advice to anyone thinking about buying a newly built house is, don't do it.

This is not to say that a new house cannot have a fascination of its own. New surroundings and a different atmosphere can be exciting and stimulating, and taking over ownership of a well-cared-for, seasoned house and remodeling it to fit your specific wants and needs can be enormously satisfying. Unfortunately, all too often we only move our old environment to a new location.

Even more revealing than a person's face, houses reflect the character of the people who live in them. In an established development, look at three houses which were all alike when first occupied. One will need painting badly. There may be a rusting automobile in the backyard, broken toys on the crabgrass, garbage cans in full view. This house has only been occupied and used, not lived in or cared for, and it will probably continue to decay and be a bad neighbor.

Another house may be neat enough, with the so-called foundation planting just as it was when stuck there by the builder. The ungainly picture window displays an equally ungainly but familiar lamp, and the front door is covered with the standard ugly aluminum storm door. The house is lived in, but only joylessly maintained in a way that prevents it from becoming anything more than a house—its identity as a home lost in rigid conformity.

The third house, which looked like the other two when built, is now a home and a valuable investment. The monotonous picture window has been removed to provide privacy from the street, and a carefully scaled entrance welcomes you. A fireplace has been added to invite quiet conversation and reading instead of television, dormers have expanded the attic, and the garden is nicely designed and well tended. It is not difficult to decide which family you would rather know and would prize as friends and neighbors.

But it is not only in suburban areas that remodeling is important. In every town and city, you will see sturdy old buildings and houses with their windows boarded up, standing behind overgrown hedges and weed-choked lawns, or sidewalks blocked by garbage dumped there by the cramped occupants of nearby apartment complexes to await the once-a-week trash collection. These buildings may be beyond repair, but more often their abandonment by absentee landlords is simply an appalling waste. Intelligent remodeling can not only make the buildings habitable, but restore entire neighborhoods to being valuable assets of the city. Georgetown, in the District of Columbia, is perhaps the most famous example of what can be accomplished through astute remodeling.

Before and during World War II, Georgetown was practically a disaster area, something you made a point of looking away from on the way to the Capitol. Now it is one of the best neighborhoods in Washington. This transformation was not brought about by a powerful government agency of highly paid experts working in committee, but by individual homeowners working by themselves and with their neighbors to improve their homes.

Remodeling is important. The Kleenex-culture in our country has ended and we can no longer afford to throw things away after a short use, only adding to the litter seen everywhere. The same is true of our houses.

Remodeling is also important in the cities, where
run-down but solidly-built houses (top) can be
turned into attractive and desirable homes.

A. J. Harmon, A.I.A.

Remodeling is the first step in saving individual homes, and thereby whole streets, blocks, and neighborhoods.

As an architect, I spent many years designing large architectural projects throughout the world, but fifteen years ago I decided that I could make a more meaningful contribution to my profession by helping homeowners create economical solutions in their everyday environment, their homes. The photographs and drawings I have used to illustrate this book and my earlier work, *The Guide to Home Remodeling*, published in 1966, are ac-

tual solutions to problems worked out with private clients.

How and where we live shapes our lives and the lives of those around us. Your house should be more than simply a place to come into out of the rain. It should be a pleasant and ever changing escape from the pressures and frustrations just beyond the door. We cannot design the world around us from the ground up, but we can start with what we have, our homes, because they are what influence our lives, our neighborhoods, our cities, and our world.

2
Contract and Legal Regulations

Not all areas and towns in the United States have laws in the form of zoning ordinances and building codes that regulate construction, but most do, and you must comply with the regulations. Cities, townships, and villages have set requirements governing the construction of any new structures or the alteration of existing buildings and houses. These regulations are designed to protect you, your family, and your property. So before you begin thinking about your remodeling seriously, investigate the deed restrictions, zoning ordinances, and building codes in your area.

Deed Restrictions

A deed restriction is a condition written into the deed to your property to protect you and your neighbors from unwanted alterations and to maintain a level of excellence in the neighborhood. Since it may supersede less strict zoning ordinances, you should reread your deed carefully before you plan your remodeling. Deed restrictions can limit the use of certain materials, the type of construction, the area in which you can expand your house, the height of additions, and even the kind of roof you may have.

Building restrictions in the deed may state that all new construction and any additions to your house must be built of brick. They may limit the size of the windows or the color of the exterior—for example, they may prohibit you from constructing vast expanses of glass walls, and your neighbor from painting his house a shocking pink with purple trim.

You may be prohibited from using a flat or a shed roof on an addition or from building with exposed concrete block, structural steel, or corrugated metal. A clause may even prevent you from placing a prefabricated toolhouse or garden house on your property.

The area in which you are permitted to build an addition may be restricted to the rear of the house or to any one side. You may not be allowed to add a garage in front, or if you are, you may not be permitted to have the garage doors facing toward the street. Construction may be limited to no more than a small percentage of the site so that a large portion of the property remains free. A deed restriction can prevent you from building an addition or adding a second floor to your house if it blocks your neighbor's view.

The style of architecture of the remodeling may have to conform to that already existing in the neighborhood—for example, your addition might have to be Spanish or American Colonial. Far-out modern or novel architectural styles may be prohibited, meaning you cannot remodel a house in the flat-roofed, glass-walled, Bauhaus style when all the other houses in the neighborhood are Cape Cod cottages.

Deed restrictions are designed to maintain the character of the neighborhood. They may be dogmatic, but with intelligent interpretation they may also be responsible for creating a neighborhood of consistency, with stabilized property values.

Zoning Ordinances

Zoning ordinances restrict and define the use of land and buildings for residences, business, and industry. Unlike deed restrictions, these ordinances are almost always written for your protection to prevent the conversion of the property next to or across the street from you into a gasoline station, trailer park, or anything else that would diminish the value of your home as a residence. Ordinances also regulate the number of families allowed to live in one house. Some ordinances permit two-family homes, while others may allow you to rent out an apartment in your home only if you are also in residence as the owner. These ordinances are meant to protect the neighborhood from rooming houses that might strain the water supply, sewage systems, and municipal services. Some areas are so strictly zoned that only one family, and a single kitchen, are permitted on the site, so if you are considering converting your garage into an apartment, check the local zoning ordinances first.

The percentage of the site that can be built on will be regulated, along with minimum front, side, and back yards. The height of hedges and fences may also be limited so that pedestrians and traffic are not endangered at blind corners.

Zoning prevents the construction of chicken coops, stables, outhouses, billboards, or anything that might constitute a neighborhood nuisance. Parking is usually regulated so that the street will not be blocked by cars that prevent a fire truck or an ambulance from getting to someone's home in case of emergency.

A copy of the zoning ordinance is usually available at the town hall or building inspector's office. You should get a copy and familiarize yourself with it before you begin to plan your remodeling because unless you obtain a variance beforehand, any illegal structure may be removed and you may be subject to a fine.

Variance

If you feel that you are being too tightly restricted by a particular ordinance, you may apply to your town's zoning board to have the ordinance waived. This waiver is called a variance.

The zoning in your area, for instance, may require that a side yard from the lot line to any structure be 15 feet, while you want to add a room that would leave a side yard of only 14 feet. The zoning board of appeals meets periodically to review just such cases and your application would come before it. You must announce your intentions to your neighbors, and then a public meeting is called. If anyone objects to your proposal, he is given a chance to voice his objections at the meeting and a solution is usually worked out to everyone's satisfaction.

Building Codes

Just as each district of a town is regulated by a zoning ordinance, each building within that district must conform to a building code which is designed to protect public health and safety. For private residences, the code stipulates the size and quality of the beams that support a floor or a roof and the minimum size of structural columns, walls, and footings. It may control the design of roofs to prevent them from collapsing under a snow load or blowing off in a high wind. The code also regulates the construction of chimneys, the installation of furnaces, and the storage of fuel so that homes do not become firetraps.

Plumbing systems are also regulated to ensure that sanitary conditions will be sufficient to protect you and your family, not only in your own home, but also from faulty plumbing problems due to a neighbor's negligence. All electrical work is governed by the code and, as with the plumbing system, is overseen by a building inspector during the remodeling to protect you from electric shock and fires caused by faulty wiring.

The building code establishes only minimum safety standards. It requires that any plumbers and electricians you hire be licensed and, if your remodeling is extensive enough to require a building permit, that they take out separate permits for their work. Some areas allow you to do the plumbing and electrical work on your own house. If you plan to do your own work, get a copy of the code and conform to it. The building code was instituted for your protection; building inspectors are not obstacles to be circumvented.

Building Inspector

If you or your contractor is required to obtain a building permit, a building inspector must be called in to approve each stage of the work. For instance, he must see to it that the wiring is properly installed before it is covered over with new wall surfaces. If you do not need a building permit and are going to do the work yourself, the building inspector can be of great help in advising you on the best and safest way to do things. Before you start tearing out walls or running wires for a new electrical outlet, ask his opinion and follow his advice.

Building Permit

Extensive remodeling requires a building permit, and the owner or contractor who is to do the work must apply for one. Drawings of the proposed changes must be submitted to the building department and checked to see that everything you propose to do conforms to the zoning ordinances and the building code. During the remodeling, a building inspector will periodically investigate the work to ensure that it is proceeding in accordance with the drawings he has on file in his office. If it is not, he will require the contractor to redo any work that is not properly done.

If you plan to do the work yourself, you may need a building permit for any major structural changes or additions that require the installation of new plumbing or wiring. Adding a sliding glass door, putting in a bay window, finishing off the attic or basement, putting on a new roof, enclosing an existing porch, or putting in new appliances probably would not require a permit because this type of remodeling is inside the existing structure. Adding a porch, room, fireplace, garage, or changing the garage into living quarters, however, would require a building permit and you would not be allowed to use the new space until the building inspector issues a Certificate of Occupancy (usually referred to simply as a C.O.).

If you are in doubt as to whether you do or do not need a building permit for your remodeling, consult the building department in your town hall. Getting a permit takes about a week, and you will be asked to pay a fee based on the cost of construction.

Certificate of Occupancy

The Certificate of Occupancy is issued only after the building inspector has approved each stage of the remodeling and is satisfied that it has been completed according to the plans filed with his office when the building permit was issued. This protects you and your neighbors from unsafe building practices. A copy of the C.O. is also sent to the tax department, so you may expect the increased value of your home due to the remodeling to be reflected in an increase in your property taxes the following year.

3
The Work–Who Will Do It, How to Get It Done

Remodeling a house is a little like altering clothes to fit—letting out the seams (adding a room or two when space gets tight), taking up hems (installing larger basement windows to allow light and air into the new recreation room), redyeing (applying a fresh coat of paint and new roofing shingles), restyling (putting in a bay window and a new circular driveway). Yet many people who are incapable of doing more than sewing on a button (replacing a broken windowpane), and would be embarrassed to wear ill-fitting home-altered clothes, seem to have no compunctions about cutting apart and patching together their houses without any previous training or experience in home design. Strangely enough, living in a grotesque and misshapen home does not seem to bother them. Anyone would feel hesitant about cutting into a fabric that costs $90 a square yard. But most homes cost more than twice that amount per square yard. Think about it.

The Architect

The architect is to remodeling what the general practitioner is to medicine—both are expert at finding out what is wrong and how to fix it. The difference is that architects must often make house calls to examine their patients, for they must determine the general condition of your house and the property around it, and what is wrong with both, in order to advise you on present and future improvements. An architect will not necessarily save you money because he will work within the budget you set up, but he will see that you get the most for your money and that it is wisely spent for what is best for your house and your family's way of living. He can organize, plan, design, do the drawings needed, and supervise the remodeling whether you hire a contractor or do the work yourself and only need advice on the most efficient way to proceed with the least expensive materials. If you do require some outside help, he will know the most reputable contractors for specific jobs.

The amount you have to spend does not determine whether you need the services of an architect. You could spend $300 putting in a new sliding glass door only to realize afterward that you have ruined the facade of your house—that for $12.00 more you could have had insulated glass installed. You could spend $3,000 adding a porch and discover later that it keeps the sun from warming the living room in winter, that it is damp in spring, and gets no cooling breeze in summer.

The best way to find out if you need an architect to do a specific job is to ask him. He will not charge you for simply talking to him. Usually you can decide for yourself what remodeling is most important to you and your family and where you want to concentrate your efforts, just as when you go to a doctor, you tell him where it hurts so that he can come up with the proper diagnosis and cure. But if your house "aches all over," you will need an architect to tell you what is the matter with it and how to correct it.

Working with an Architect

It is important to find an architect you can work with on a person-to-person basis. This is not always easy. You might call or write the local chapter of The American Institute of Architects (A.I.A.) and ask for the names of members in your area who do residential work. You can also look up registered architects in the Yellow Pages and call those nearby. Tell each architect your problem over the telephone, and if he is interested (some architects will not take on a remodeling job), go to see him. Consult several architects and choose the one who seems the most interested in helping you develop your ideas.

On the first go-round, it will help the architect and save you money if you draw up a rough floor plan and take it, along with photographs of the house, to his office. He might be able to show you with a quick sketch the best way to solve your problem. Or you might do your own remodeling design and ask him to criticize it and suggest changes. This is a good way to indicate to him what you would like done and where. It also will give him an idea of the scope of the work so that he can make an intelligent estimate of how much it will cost. He may charge you if he spends much time giving you advice or sketches. Do not expect him to work for nothing; ask his rate first. Also ask who the best contractors and subcontractors are in your area. He will know because he will have worked with many of them. He can not only tell you who would be best to hire, but more importantly, who *not* to let into your house.

If you are going to do all the work yourself, perhaps all you will need from the architect is a quick sketch to get you started in the right direction. If more work than that is required, he will frankly discuss his fee and what you will get for the amount you pay him.

An architect's fee is usually based on a percentage of the cost of the work, but he may also be paid a set fee established in advance, or by the hour. On small jobs, your contract with the architect may consist of a simple letter of agreement, but on more extensive work a standard A.I.A. contract covering all contingencies is better.

If a general contractor is to do the work, the architect will measure the existing house, draw sketches of what you would like done until you are happy with the solution, and then do preliminary drawings to get estimates from several contractors on how much the work will cost. Preliminary bids are usually too high, so you and your architect must sit down together and decide what to eliminate, where to cut corners, and what to simplify. A second preliminary bid is then requested from the contractor you have decided to use. If this falls close to the budget you have worked out, a final set of working drawings is made and given to the contractor for a final price. The architect will settle the contract between you and the contractor. It is usually the standard form of agreement issued by the A.I.A.

It is always better for the architect to supervise the remodeling, because as the work progresses, there will be problems that could not be foreseen: old foundation walls and wells where you wanted to excavate for an addition; beams and joists that turn up unexpectedly when the walls are uncovered; delivery of the wrong material or equipment when returning it could create delays. However, if it is not a complicated job and you think you are knowledgeable enough to oversee the work yourself, you will be able to save money by doing so.

The Contractor

You may not need a general contractor. If you have found an architect, ask him if between you, you cannot schedule the work and supervise the subcontractors. Contractors are not licensed. Anyone can hang out a sign and become a contractor, and few have any conception of planning or design. The contractor's job is simply to coordinate the work of carpenters and subcontractors, getting materials and labor to the remodeling site at approximately the right time. A competent and reliable contractor can get the work completed quickly and with a minimum of frustration. Unfortunately, the owner or architect all too often ends up doing a good part of the work because the contractor is lax or incompetent.

If you do not have an architect and cannot do the work yourself, finding a good contractor may take months. Many will not consider small remodeling jobs. Firms specializing in kitchens, basements, dormers, or porches rarely can remodel to suit your specific wants and needs. They tend to give you what *they* can do instead of what *you* want done.

You can call local architects and ask for recommendations, but they may be reluctant to give you the names of their best people since good contractors are hard to find and are booked up long in advance. It is better to prepare first a list of possible contractors and then ask the architects which one they feel would be best.

The Better Business Bureau is usually a poor agency to consult when checking on a contractor. They can tell you if any complaints have been lodged against one of their own members, but since joining the organization is not compulsory, it's unlikely they will be able to tell you even this much about most contractors. A better source would be your lawyer or someone who works at the local courthouse. Such an individual is more likely to know who has been sued lately, and how often. Good contractors seldom have to go to court, while incompetent ones spend a lot of time there.

You can also call lumberyards and building supply companies for names, but since they depend on contractors for a great deal of their business, you are not going to hear anything bad about a contractor from them.

Banks can be a good source of reference, as can the local building department. But they, too, usually abstain from saying anything unfavorable for fear of offending someone. You might try real estate agents, since they have no ax to grind and know what is going on, but few are able to judge a good contractor from a bad one except on hearsay.

After you have the names of as many contracting firms as you can find, go around to their offices. If a general contractor works out of his home without an office or a secretary, it is best to forget him—especially if he just rents his house. You could go back tomorrow and find he has moved out of town. He should have an office, a secretary (not an answering service) to take messages, storage space and a shop for woodworking, and his own home—and he should have been in business in the same community for five to ten years (the longer the better).

Do not worry if his office is a bit shabby and threadbare. A good contractor is too busy working to do much about fixing up his own office. If his office is impressively decorated with wall-to-wall carpeting and walnut paneling and features canned music, leave. The good impression is what you will be paying for if you hire him, not his work.

Get his bank references (the mortgage banks and finance companies that handle his installment loans) and check on them. Find out where he is doing work at the present time and go and investigate, not just the workmanship, but also the workmen. They are the ones who will be spending a lot of time in your home, not the general contractor, who will be busy elsewhere most of the time. If possible, talk with the homeowner and find out if the men are prompt, quiet, and clean up every evening before they leave the job.

Make sure the contractor carries workmen's compensation, public liability, and property damage insurance, then call his insurance agent and ask how claims are handled.

Once you find two or three contractors you

believe you can trust in your home, make appointments for them to come to your house at a certain time. Promptness is important; if a contractor is not on time for an interview, he will probably not be on time with his work. If he does not call to tell you he will be delayed, it is best not to deal with him. Get the names of architects the contractor has worked for in the past and ask which one he can recommend to help you with the design. Generally, contractors who have worked for architects do better work than those who have not, and some may even be able to help you plan the remodeling.

The contractor should be able to help you measure the dimensions of your house and draw up a plan of the changes to be made. He should then give you an accurate estimate of the cost and tell you whether or not you need a building permit. Ask him to itemize everything in as much detail as possible: height, width, depth, color, finish, brand name, and model number. He should also specify the length of time his bid is good for, and when he can begin and end the work.

Get this kind of estimate from two or three contractors if you can, and let each one know you are getting bids from others. If anyone objects to doing this amount of work before he knows he has the job, ask him if he can suggest any other way for you to get the best job for the least amount of money. If he gets angry and walks away, forget him.

Choose the contractor you think you will get along with best, the one who will work with you. The lowest bid may not be the best bargain if it comes from a contractor you do not like. Discuss it with the contractor you prefer and see if he can meet the price. The low bid could come from a man who wants the work so badly that he has underestimated the cost in order to ensure getting the job. He may do unsatisfactory work, use poor materials, or simply quit when cost problems mount, leaving you with a torn-apart house. The highest bid will not ensure you of the best job either. It may be so high because the contractor really does not want to do the work.

Once you have chosen a contractor, have a contract drawn up by your lawyer which includes the specifications and dated drawings, or use the A.I.A. form supplied by your architect. Do not sign a contract made up by the contractor's lawyer before having another lawyer, one who is familiar with this type of work, go over it. Get everything in writing. Do not agree to anything verbally.

Working with a Contractor

After you have decided on a contractor and have signed the contract, ask him for a work schedule so you will know when his men will arrive, what they will be working on, and for how long. It is essential to know when the plumbing and electricity will be turned off so you can make other arrangements.

A contractor is not a moving company, so clear the areas in which the men will be working of furniture and bric-a-brac. Cover with drop cloths beds or chairs that cannot be moved. Do not follow the contractor or his men around, asking questions or making changes in the plans, unless he has asked you to and has explained why it is necessary. Keep children and pets away from the workmen, in a separate room if possible, and never ask the men to answer the phone or keep an eye on the youngsters while you run to town.

Be prepared for a lot of dirt, sawdust, noise, and changes. Have in mind alternatives for everything in case there is a shortage or a long delay in delivery of anything from paneling to toilets.

Pay the contractor according to the contract—but only for labor, materials that have been installed, and work completed. Make no exceptions, no matter what the reason or excuse. Signed contract aside, your only hold over the contractor is the money you owe him. Once he has been paid, only his ethics will keep him on the job or prompt him to return to fix leaking windows and chimneys or other work that may have gone wrong—and it is safer not to have to rely on your impression of his character.

If you cannot find a general contractor you feel you can trust in your home, you can get your remodeling done by hiring your own subcontractors.

Subcontractors

Subcontractors, usually hired by the general contractor, are the electrician, plumber, heating and air conditioning installers, mason, spackler, painter, weatherstripper, and tile setter. You can hire them easily, but you must be prepared to wait until they can fit your smaller job in between the larger ones they have with general contractors and builders. They depend on them for work continually, while they may work only once for you.

A contractor may subcontract out all of the work, but usually he maintains a small crew of carpenters, who come in two categories: rough carpenters (sometimes called lumpers), who do the rough work—the framing, roofing, siding, and plywood sheathing—and finish carpenters, who do the trim, set doors and windows, box out columns, and build bookcases and kitchen cabinets.

If you are going to act as your own contractor, the best place to begin is with a good carpenter. He will have worked with all the other trades and will often know the right people to do the best job for you. A good carpenter is harder to find than a good contractor, and because carpenters are in demand, they are expensive. A good carpenter can help you coordinate the other work, but since this is not his real job, be prepared for some mistakes. Have a written contract drawn up with him. Do not hire him as an employee or you will be responsible for deducting state and federal withholding taxes and for paying unemployment insurance and workmen's compensation.

If you decide to handle the carpentry work yourself, you still have to locate subcontractors for the other work. The process for finding subcontractors is about the same as that for finding a general contractor, except that many subcontractors do not have offices but work out of their homes. The only difficulty about acting as your own contractor is managing the scheduling and timing—getting the right workmen and materials together at the right place at the right time. In most cases, it will take a little longer to get the job done, but it is less expensive than hiring a contractor, especially if you are going to do some of the subcontracting work yourself.

Even if you were required to get a building permit, you may not have to hire a licensed plumber or electrician if you are working on your own house. But unless you are very capable, it is better to hire experienced professionals.

Masonry, especially in the construction of a fireplace, also requires experience because of the fire codes. And building a fireplace that does not smoke seems to be beyond the capabilities of even some top-notch masons.

If you do decide to hire subcontractors directly, have your lawyer draw up a separate contract for each one, with specifications and payments spelled out to the letter. Include references to dated plans as part of the contract.

Talk to your insurance agent to be sure you are fully covered in case anything happens to a workman or passerby on your property. You may have to fence in a storage area or lock lumber and other materials in your garage at night because even in the best of neighborhoods things have a way of disappearing. And unless there are signs of forced entry, thefts of building materials and tools are not covered by insurance.

You should increase the fire insurance on your house as the remodeling progresses, and make sure you are fully covered when the work is finished.

4
Where and How to Start

Planning

Before you do anything to any room in your home, draw up a floor plan of the entire house. It will be the basis for all your remodeling and all other work. A plan showing elevations will be of enormous help if you intend to get advice from an architect or contractor since it will enable him to see more clearly what you have in mind and the scope of the projected work. It will also allow him to give you an idea of some of the problems you will face and a more accurate cost estimate of the remodeling. Even if all you intend to do at present is redecorate, a good plan will help you later in ordering the correct amount of tile or paint.

To measure the house, get at least a 25-foot metal tape that rolls out of a circular case. They are available at any hardware store or lumberyard. Be sure to buy one that is marked in feet and inches. One marked only in inches can lead to mistakes, as will a shorter tape that requires you to mark the wall and remeasure every few feet.

Use a large piece of paper or cardboard to draw on so you can leave plenty of space between the measurements you write down or they will get confused. Make a rough drawing of each floor, using a double line for the walls and partitions, one line for a window, and no line for a door unless there is a step there. The drawing does not have to be accurate, but it should give a general idea of projections and setbacks in the wall.

Begin by taking an overall room measurement from one wall to the opposite wall, in each direction. To measure the details in each room, begin at the most convenient corner, taking dimensions from the wall (not from the baseboard) to the first opening or projection. Have someone hold the end of the tape at the corners while you measure to the window and door openings (*not* the outside edge of the trim). If someone holds the tape in the corner while you pull out the entire length of the tape, it will be a more accurate measurement. If you measure one bit of wall to a window, then measure the width of the window and move on to measure the next wall space, you are bound to make a lot of mistakes. Measurements do not have to be any closer than to the nearest ½ inch. Draw in the door swings, electric outlets, registers

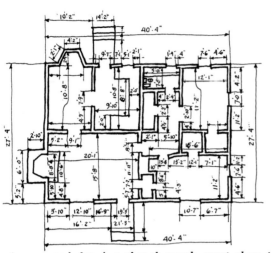
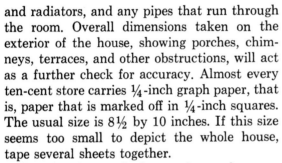
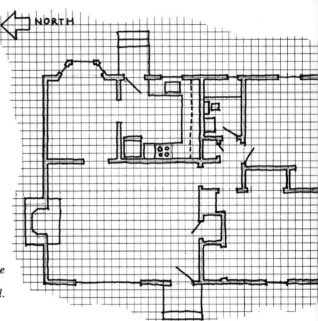

A measured drawing, though rough, must show the dimensions clearly. The scaled drawing can then give an accurate picture of the areas and footage involved. Each grid here is equal to 1 square foot.

and radiators, and any pipes that run through the room. Overall dimensions taken on the exterior of the house, showing porches, chimneys, terraces, and other obstructions, will act as a further check for accuracy. Almost every ten-cent store carries ¼-inch graph paper, that is, paper that is marked off in ¼-inch squares. The usual size is 8½ by 10 inches. If this size seems too small to depict the whole house, tape several sheets together.

Transfer the rough plan to the graph paper, letting each square equal 1 square foot. Proportion as carefully as you can and try to get the overall dimensions as accurately as possible, although small mistakes are not too important unless they occur in a kitchen or bathroom where cabinets and fixture sizes must be exact.

With the plan in front of you, make a list of all the things you think are wrong with each room and what might be done to correct them. Remodeling possibilities depend on your house, its location, your family, and the way you want to live. If you want a new kitchen but need another bedroom, it is better to satisfy the need before the want.

It is also unwise to concentrate your entire budget on one particular room, such as the kitchen, if other areas of the house cannot be brought up to a similar level of improvement. Do not put a new $5,000 kitchen in a $15,000 house. This is called "overbuilding." If you can spend $5,000, it is better to put in a

$2,500 kitchen and use the rest of the money to improve other rooms.

It is also important to avoid overbuilding for your neighborhood. You do not want to invest more in your home than you could ever hope to get for it if forced to sell. Much depends on your neighbors. Take a good look at their houses and compare them to yours. Check with a few real estate people before you decide how much you can safely invest. If you are told your neighbors' houses are worth $25,000 and you only paid $18,000 in yours, invest the $7,000 difference in remodeling if necessary. But if their houses are only worth about $18,000 and you have already invested $25,000 in yours, I suggest you think twice about extensive remodeling.

Designing

The success or failure of every remodeling depends on the design and planning. This is the road map to follow to get you from your starting point to where you want to go. Some people manage to get from Maine to Florida without a map, but it can be an expensive and time-consuming trip by way of Chicago. And, just as an automobile is not much good without seats, your home is at a disadvantage if your furniture will not fit in it comfortably.

Measure each piece of furniture in the rooms that you are going to be remodeling. Using a scale of ¼ inch to the foot (the same as the measured plan of the house), draw and cut out of cardboard beds, end tables, sofa, chairs, chests, tables, and desks and "play house" with your floor plan. It is a lot easier on your back to check the fit by moving little cardboard pieces around on the plan than by moving a bed or sofa from one wall to the other.

A sofa may be in front of a window, but a bed should not be. Even a high window can cause cold downdrafts, and if the window is left open during the summer, a sudden rain could soak the mattress. Beds should be placed against inside walls, if possible, but if that means you will fall over them when you enter the room, you may be forced to place them on an outside wall. (See the sections on individual rooms for specifics on furniture placement.)

Using the pieces of cardboard, place the furniture so that you can move easily through the rooms and so that electrical outlets, radiators, and registers are not lost behind a breakfront or a sofa. Make sure no furniture blocks door swings. Any new electric outlets should be placed where you need them, eliminating the use of extension cords. Make a note of everything that is wrong with the furniture placement in each room in your house so you can correct these faults as you remodel. Are the beds difficult to make because of tight space? Is there enough light and privacy in each room? Can you see the kitchen sink from the hallway, dining room, or living room? Can you look into the bathroom from the living room or dining room? Is the dining room too small to be useful, or is it used only on Thanksgiving, Christmas, and special occasions? Is there a linen closet? Is there a guest and coat closet handy to the front and back doors? Are the front and back doors protected from snow and rain, or do you get soaked as you fumble for the key?

All of these inconveniences are the result of bad planning and should not have been allowed in the first place, but they can be corrected if the remodeling is properly designed.

Begin the designing by including everything you have always wanted. Many times it is a mistake not to complete some of your future dreams in the present. You may be surprised how little they cost to incorporate while you are doing something else that seems unrelated. They might cost less in the future, but in the meantime you will be enjoying them. If you are planning to panel the living room and buy a new sofa, but have always dreamed of having a bay window, forget the sofa and put in the bay window with a big built-in window seat; nobody ever sits in the middle of a sofa anyway.

It is always a mistake, however, to spend more on a house than you can comfortably afford. If you are constantly striving to meet payments on new improvements, the joy of having them will quickly disappear and you will even begin to resent them.

The advantage of making an inclusive plan with everything you want is that you can then eliminate the more impractical, expensive things that you can live without, and readjust the plan until it contains only those elements you must have and those you really want.

When designing additions, use dimensions of 4 feet. Most studs and joists are placed on 16-inch centers, and all lumber—finishing and rough plywood, paneling, Sheetrock—and most carpeting are manufactured in sizes divisible by 4. An addition that is 10 feet 7¾ inches wide and 14 feet 8½ inches long will cost more to build than one 12 feet wide and 16 feet long. Concrete block comes in a dimension of 15 feet ⅝ inches, so that when mortar is added, the center line of the mortar for three blocks is 4 feet. Other sizes are available, but they are either 8 or 12 inches in length at the mortar center line.

Timing

The timing of remodeling can be important because of weather conditions. If you time things correctly, you may be able to get help when it costs less. Therefore you should plan and design your remodeling at least a year in advance of the actual start of construction. In the North, I would not start knocking down an outside wall between Christmas and New Year's—in fact, that is the worst week to get anything accomplished anywhere—but most carpenters are not as busy in the winter and early spring as they are the rest of the year and may charge less for inside work during the cold months. Concrete work and masonry, especially foundations, should be done only after the ground has thawed in the spring, that is, after all danger of frost is past.

There are ways of doing masonry during freezing weather, but they cost more and are used mainly in public and commercial work. Late fall is a good time to have concrete terraces and footings poured because most people will not think of doing them until spring.

Once footings and foundation walls are in, the rough carpenters will erect the framing and do the closing in very quickly. On a small one-room addition, a week should be more than ample time. Showers are not much of a problem because canvas can be nailed over the opening to the existing house. However, do not expect carpenters to use power tools or saw wet wood in the rain. Framing and exterior-grade plywood will not be damaged by rain after it is on the walls and floors, but the finished roof should be on before you let the addition weather the winter. Interior-grade plywood, plaster board, and paneling should not be allowed to get wet or they will delaminate.

Interior painting, staining, and floor refinishing should be done when it is warm so that the windows can be left open for ventilation. Some of the new paints and varnishes are not too offensive, but the plastic-based finishes produce toxic fumes. Others are highly inflammable while drying. Mastic for floor tile is inflammable, too, so be careful about smoking in the room and leave the windows open for fresh air. No matter what finish you use, always follow the manufacturer's instructions on the label.

Scheduling

Scheduling the various workmen so that they will be able to do their work without getting in each other's way or damaging completed work requires careful planning.

Masonry work in the form of footings and foundation walls is done first—unless you want to have the soil termite-proofed, which is done before the concrete is poured. No one can do much of anything until the concrete is finished and has cured for about a week, although some rough plumbing and drains can be begun.

Rough carpentry is the next logical step, and the framing, including sheathing and roofing, goes quickly. Next in line are the plumber and electrician, who will do only the roughing in, which must be approved by the building inspector before the plumbing and wiring lines are covered by dry wall. Finished siding, insulation, doors, and windows are then put in place, followed by any heating or air conditioning ductwork that is required. With the installation of the doors and windows, the remodeling is closed in and the finish work can go ahead. The more of the finish work you can do yourself, the more money you can save because it is here that construction gets expensive. Except for the plumbing and electric work and, possibly, the spackling and carpet laying, no special talent or education is needed. So if you passed the birdhouse and magazine-rack phase in high-school manual training, or consider yourself "handy," you can save money by doing the finishing work. Who cares if a few impressions of a hammer head find their way into window trim that will be covered by drapery anyway? It is much better to spend the money on a good design.

The trim around the door and windows, baseboards, and any other carpentry should not be started until after the third coat of spackle is on. Finish plumbing and electrical work may be completed unless there is to be ceramic tile on the bathroom floor. In that case, the plumber would return and set the fixtures on top of the tile. The bathtub will have been installed as the framing was being done for a snug fit. If you can hold off tile work in the bathroom for four to six months, you can avoid having small cracks in the grout at the corners and the top of the tub because by then most of the settling of the structure will have taken place.

When the remodeling is ready for painting, the wood trim should be given a coat of sealer and two coats of paint. If stain is used, the primer should be omitted and two coats of varnish applied. The Sheetrock should be given two coats of paint. Tile floors in the kitchen are laid after the cabinets are installed. Wall-to-wall carpeting is the last thing to be put in.

5
How to Economize— and Where *Not* To

The first and most important step toward getting the most for your money in remodeling is to get the best plan and design you can devise or have made for you. Then stick to them. This is especially important if you are going to be doing the work a step at a time. Each step should be complete in itself and an integrated part of the final design.

If you are not sure what you want, obviously you will not be able to work it out yourself. Do not be tempted to economize; go to a professional for help. Planning and design are more important in remodeling than money. Only the wealthy can afford to change their minds and have things done over if they are not satisfied. It is better to pay an architect for a good design than to pay workmen to labor for weeks in areas and on rooms that will not be suitable when finished and do not increase the value of your house.

Reuse and Reorganize

One way a design may be economical is in reusing existing space and reorganizing the circulation within the house so that areas are utilized more efficiently. Almost every house has at least one or two spaces that are not being used to their full potential, whether it is a bedroom almost, but not quite, large enough to serve double duty as a quiet study, or a basement that could be used for something besides storage if it were not so dark and dreary. Maybe a bay window projected over the foundation will increase the size of the bedroom enough so that you can place several extra chairs and a small desk in it. Larger windows and even terraces can be built off basements to make them into really attractive and usable rooms.

New Space

If no one uses the front door because the back door or side door is more convenient, close off the unused door and make a new entrance on the back or side of the house next to the driveway. This is an especially good idea if the front door opens into the living room. By changing it, you can improve the circulation and have a cleaner and quieter house.

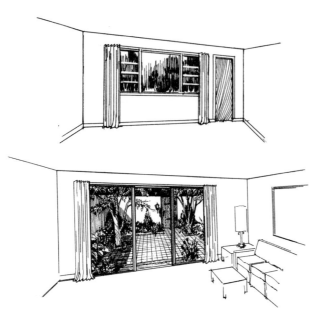

A picture window (top) *changed to sliding glass doors facing a walled garden eliminates the front door entrance into the living room.*

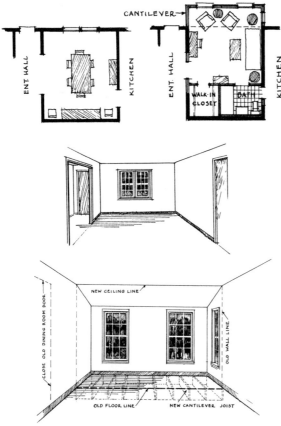

Cantilevering gains floor space to change a dining room into a guest room or study.

Be cautious about closing in a porch to make it into living space because porches were often constructed to protect the inside rooms from the weather. Once they are made into rooms, they may still be used only as hallways, and will cut off light and air from the other interior rooms. However, if the porch is in good condition, is of sufficient size, and is located where it would make a valuable room, by all means consider enclosing it. You will not have to go to the expense of building new foundations and a roof, and since most building codes do not require a building permit for enclosing a porch, the chances are that your property taxes will not be increased.

For safety, every house should have exits at opposite sides. There is nothing wrong with an entrance that has a country kitchen atmosphere, if it is properly designed. You might make the picture window in the living room into sliding glass doors facing a private walled courtyard that can become part of the living room in the summer.

Many people with family rooms find they use their dining room only twice a year—at Thanksgiving and Christmas. An unused dining room is a very economical space to convert to a study or guest room by adding a bath or lavatory because the kitchen plumbing is close by and can usually be extended without any problem.

You can create additional space by cantilevering floors and ceilings out over the foundations. This way you can avoid the extra expense of new footings and foundation walls. There would have to be a beam to support the roof, since outside walls are structural. But much of the old material and windows can be reused to enclose the new space. You can easily add 2 to 3 feet to a room this way, and at the same time improve the facade of the house.

Plan a new room where there are two existing walls so you will only have to build two new walls instead of three. There will already be wiring and heat in the wall, which can possibly be connected to the new room. Of course, if it is inconvenient to place the new room where there are two walls, spend the additional money and build it in its ideal location.

The Wet Wall

Most houses have what is called a wet wall. This is the wall that contains the hot and cold plumbing pipes and drainage lines. When adding a bath, it is best to take advantage of this wet wall by placing the new bath back to back, adjacent to, or over an existing bathroom or kitchen. However, if you would have to build new hallways and cut into existing space to get to the new bathroom, it will not be much cheaper than placing the bathroom elsewhere and having additional pipe installed. There is nothing sacred about using the original plumbing, so do not try to economize here if it doesn't make good sense.

In the Kitchen

Factory-made kitchen cabinets are quite expensive, so if you are considering remodeling your kitchen, you can save money by making cabinets yourself or having them built on the job by a carpenter. If you need a lot of kitchen storage, it may be better, and far less expensive, to design a more compact kitchen with fewer cabinets and use the space saved for a pantry with simple open storage shelves which you can put up yourself. A pantry might also make an excellent back entrance and laundry. If you are buying a new refrigerator, you might want to put the old one in the pantry for extra ice, food storage, and the children's soft drinks.

Economize on new kitchen appliances by buying the simplest. Avoid so-called work-saving gadgets such as wall toasters and built-in counter blenders. Eventually they will need repairing and everything will have to be dismantled to get them out, leaving holes in your counter top or wall.

Do not buy a range that has clocks, timers, and as many complicated controls as the dashboard of a 747; there are just that many more things to go wrong, and you will not use them anyway. Stick to the simple range with an oven that has a window in the door so you can see if something is cooking properly without opening the door and losing heat.

Push-button controls on the front of the range may be dangerous. You may accidentally lean against them while getting something out of a cabinet over the cooking surface, or small children may play with them. Controls above the burners are also dangerous. It is easy to get a painful burn or catch a bathrobe sleeve on fire while reaching over a hot pan.

By all means, spend the extra money for a refrigerator on rollers so that you can slide it out to clean behind and under it and retrieve things that fall behind it. Do not invest in a refrigerator with unadjustable plastic rack holders in the back and on the sides; these pull loose after several years. Spend the extra money for a refrigerator with adjustable metal rack supports. Refrigerators with ice water and ice cube dispensers in the door may be convenient, but even those with an automatic icemaker in the freezing compartment cost more to buy, install, and operate. They also make a lot of noise and the automatic ice-maker takes up half the freezer space.

A stainless-steel sink (although far from stainless as far as water marks are concerned) is better than either enameled cast iron or steel. The enamels chip and require constant scrubbing, which will eventually wear the enamel down to the base.

A garbage disposal in the sink is a convenience that is worth the money because it saves you from carrying out soggy garbage. Some codes do require a separate septic tank for them, however, so check the regulations in your area before you buy.

Dishwashers do get glasses, plates, and silver spotless, and many people feel they cannot live without them. They are not too expensive to buy if you choose the simplest, which is usually the best, but they do use a great deal of water and electricity. Even if you cannot afford a dishwasher now, it is a good idea to leave space for it when you are designing a new kitchen, and have the kitchen plumbed and wired for a later installation.

A washing machine and perhaps a dryer are musts, but here again, it is important to buy the least complex with the simplest controls. I know of no one who has figured out the separate settings for soak, wash, spin, cotton, perma-press, spin-dry, no-iron, delicate, heavy, medium, and light loads, according to weight and the kind of soap used, and all these extras are just more things that could go wrong.

Buy a separate washer and dryer. The combination is a bad investment because it does less laundry, takes twice the time to do it in, and something is always wrong with either the washer or the dryer part. The small portable washers that hook up to the sink may be handy, but they have a very small capacity and do not wash well enough to justify their purchase.

Lighting

You do not have to invest in a lot of expensive lighting fixtures for the hall, bathroom, kitchen, or dining room. Simple porcelain outlets can be installed and used with decorative light bulbs available in any electrical or hardware store. In bathrooms, one light on each side of the mirror is sufficient for shaving and the bulbs may be easily changed. It can be very irritating to stand on a ladder in a narrow hall trying to undo a cheap light fixture in the ceiling to change a bulb.

Inexpensive but effective down lights can be used in the kitchen and over the table in the dining room. In the dining room, you can use a down light on a rheostat to control the amount of light, or use a very low wattage bulb to light only the table and supplement it with candles—until you can afford a crystal chandelier.

Do not economize by failing to put in three-

Porcelain light fixtures look good, are inexpensive, and are useful in halls and ceiling locations as well as bathrooms.

way switches at the top and bottom of all stairs and at each end of hallways or rooms you must pass through to get to another room. If the light can be turned on and off at separate locations, you will save yourself a lot of bumps and bruises and have a safer house. A three-way switch also makes it easier to conserve electricity.

Doors, Floors, and Walls

At the present time I know of no attractive aluminum screen and storm door. But if you are going to put in a storm door, it makes no sense to waste money on a new expensive wood-paneled front or back door that will only be covered up.

Door hardware is important because of security, and since you use it every day, it should be good-looking, sturdy, and pleasant to touch. Cheap builder's hardware will lose its finish in several years and some may work loose and fall off in your hand. Get the best mortise lock you can afford.

Do not try to get by with cheap paint, but remember that the most expensive paint is not always the best. Unknown brands on sale usually are not the bargains they seem since you may have to use twice as much to cover the same area.

Use paint to cover old wood floors until you can afford the carpet or tile you want. Vinyl asbestos tile is inexpensive but should not be used over uneven wood floors as every imperfection will show through. The tile will wear quickly over ridges, and crack where imperfections between boards are more than a fraction of an inch. Check all tile, floor coverings, and carpet for inflammability. Some burn freely, while others are self-extinguishing. Choose one that does not burn, even if it is more expensive.

Insulation is inexpensive compared to the savings it allows on heating and cooling, so do not try to economize by skimping on insulation in your walls and ceilings.

If you are going to panel over dry wall, do not go to the expense of spackling it. Paneling a room may be less expensive than putting in wallboard and painting it. Since the wallboard will not require taping and spackling, you can use small pieces more economically. And once the paneling is on, the walls will never need paint or maintenance.

6
Money–Where to Invest, How to Borrow

Spending

Only you know how much money you can spend on your home and where it should be spent to gain maximum satisfaction. Maintenance items such as a new roof or furnace should be taken care of first, even if you only plan to stay in the house three or four years, because these are basics that prospective buyers will investigate. You may be able to incorporate these improvements with some remodeling that will make the house more attractive.

If bedroom space is cramped, you might convert the garage into additional bedrooms. Finishing a garage is fairly inexpensive and, if attached, its proximity to the kitchen plumbing makes a bath less expensive to include in the design. It may be a disadvantage, however, if you have to go through the kitchen to get to the bedrooms. If you cannot convert the garage easily, a bedroom is the least expensive room to add because it involves no plumbing. Heating is simplified since bedrooms are normally kept cooler than other rooms, and usually enough heat can be drawn off the existing system. Don't skimp. A room 12 by 16 feet costs very little more than one 10 by 14 feet.

A bathroom is an expensive room to add because of the plumbing, heating, electricity, tile, and fixtures needed. These all increase the cost a great deal in proportion to the size of the room. Building a minimum-sized structure of 5 by 7 feet will cost just as much as a more spacious bath of 8 by 8 feet. The new bathroom will be less expensive to construct if you can use the existing plumbing stack of an existing bathroom.

The kitchen is the most expensive room in the house to remodel because of the plumbing, heating, electrical and cabinet work needed, plus the appliances. Unless you plan to live in the house six to eight years, it may be a mistake to install a custom-made high-fashion kitchen. Everyone has his own way of working in a kitchen, and your way may not be suitable for someone else. This does not mean you should not make the kitchen more attractive and workable, but if your stay is indefinite, it is better to keep costs to a minimum.

Financing

It is best to pay for remodeling outright, though there are instances in which this would not be true, depending on interest rates and where your money is invested. The amount you can borrow to remodel your home will depend on your house, income, and credit standing. To get a loan, you will need a set of plans and specifications showing how you plan to remodel your home. Start looking with your own bank and then compare its loan rates and terms with those of other banks. Regulations, rates, and terms change regularly, as do different banks' lending policies.

Home Improvement Loan: These are sought by most banks because of their high yield. They are nonsecured loans, meaning there are no liens placed against the property or improvements unless the loan goes into default. The bank may send a man to inspect the property and return periodically to see if the money is being spent according to the agreement. Interest rates vary from 8 to 12 percent on a government-controlled loan of $10,000, with up to ten years to pay off.

Mortgage Loan: These can be given by a bank if you do not already have a mortgage on the property. The interest rate at this writing is between 8 and 10 percent. The amount of the mortgage will depend on the property, what you plan to do with it, and your financial situation.

Mortgage Refinancing: If you already have a mortgage on your home, you can negotiate for a new one. Refinancing will be expensive because the old mortgage must be paid off and a new one drawn up, which involves a lawyer's fee, bank charges, and probably a much higher interest rate than you pay at present.

FHA (Title I) Loan: This type of loan, taken out through a regular bank, is available only to those who can qualify for it. If your income is low and your financial situation is such that a bank does not want to lend you money, the Federal Housing Agency may guarantee payment to the bank. The bank will then lend you the money without risk. Not all banks will handle FHA loans. The maximum amount you can borrow currently is $2,500, with an interest rate of 9½ percent, but these amounts are subject to change.

FHA (K) Loan: The Federal Housing Agency must also approve these loans. They are available at 6 percent interest for a minimum loan of $2,500 and a maximum of $10,000, with twenty years to pay. However, there are additional fee payments for insurance, service charges, and FHA appraisal and inspection as the work progresses.

Open-End Mortgage Loan: If you have an open-end mortgage, you can use it to finance remodeling work. This type of mortgage provides that you may borrow as much money from the bank as you have already paid on your mortgage. Your mortgage is then increased by the amount borrowed, and the length of payment time is also increased.

Personal Loan: A commercial bank can give you a personal loan at interest rates that now vary from 12 to 18 percent. The maximum amount you can borrow is $10,000 for a minimum of three years. In spite of the high interest rates, excellent credit and references are required.

Finance Company Loan: This type of loan also has the very high interest rate of 12 to 18 percent, but the maximum is $2,500. Almost anyone can get these loans (they are also extended for automobile, television, and furniture purchases). High-pressure home-improvement salesmen will try to get you to sign finance company forms to pay for work they want you to let their company do on your house, which can be anything from basement remodeling to dormers in the attic. Never sign anything without having your lawyer or bank look it over first.

Credit Union Loan: Credit unions are a good source of money if you belong to one and the remodeling on your home is not extensive. Their terms and rates are usually generous, although there is a limit to the amount you can borrow.

Insurance Company Loan: Another way you may be able to finance your remodeling is by borrowing on your insurance. However, with any loan, read the fine print and get advice from your bank concerning the hidden costs, add-on charges, and the true amount of interest you will be paying.

7
Remodeling–Outside and Inside, Top to Bottom

In design, there is no such thing as good or bad taste. What people refer to as "taste" is nothing more than a guess at what to do with the design of a garden, house, or room. When you know what you are doing, you do not have to guess. If no one ever learned to drive an automobile properly, our highways would be a shambles. The average homeowner's refusal to learn is what is wrong with so many houses. People do not distinguish between the right and wrong way to remodel, but instead rely on guesswork and their own personal judgment—which can be good, bad, or indifferent. In this chapter I will take you from the street through every room in the house, from the attic to the basement, and give you some guidelines for remodeling so that you will not have to depend on guesswork for a successful result.

Landscaping

Any time you plant a package of seeds or set out this year's balled Christmas tree you are landscaping. Landscaping alone can add to the appearance of your home by stressing the good points of the facade and covering or leading the eye away from the less attractive details. The difference between a well-landscaped house and a poorly landscaped one is the same as that between a coat that fits well and is becoming and one that is not. Landscaping is rather expensive. Over the years you can spend thousands of dollars on it without noticing, so it is best to have a long-range plan and design of what you want done in order to get the most out of the money you will spend. If you cannot decide on a design you want to develop, get the advice and services of a landscape architect who is educated in the science of horticulture and experienced in the design and planning of gardens. He can prepare a design drawing that you can follow now and in the future, as your time and finances permit.

Landscape gardeners, who have no formal education in landscaping and whose knowledge of design is limited, can also be of help in advising you as to the trees and plants that grow best in your area and what to use for foundation and other planting. They usually have a greenhouse and nursery where you can investigate various types of shrubbery. You can either plant the trees yourself or make arrangements for the nurseryman to plant them, with a guarantee that they will survive for a year or be replaced.

Foundation planting: The lines between your house and the ground should be softened by foundation planting, which hides the masonry. Your house should nestle against the site, and look as if it belonged there and nowhere else. The entrance should be emphasized, but an Early American style house should not be overplanted with tall bushy plants around the door. Early settlers cut the trees down and kept their doors clear so that there would be no place for unfriendly strangers to take cover and lie in wait for them as they came and went. Later, when more formal styles were developed, the beautifully designed and carefully executed architectural details were not covered up with plants and vines.

The hard flat planes and corners of modern architecture usually cry out for the play of shadows, the green of luxuriant plants to soften the rigid lines and temper the strong angles. However, if your foundation planting not only covers the foundation, but the windows, walls, and roof as well, you should start over. It is not always necessary to chop everything down, however. Many times shrubs

and trees can be moved to a more suitable location where they will look good and continue to grow. If you plant slow-growing, minimal-care plants and evergreens around the foundation, only a light pruning will be needed every year or two to keep them in line.

The landscaping should "frame" your house. Just as a picture frame shows a painting off to its best advantage, proper landscaping will enhance your house. The background for your home should be uncluttered—you want to see sky and trees, not buildings or other houses. Plant fast-growing trees behind the house to block the view of other homes.

Fences: You will want to plan fences and hedges to cut off a view of the street and lessen noise and dust from passing cars. A fence or hedge for security reasons or noise control, however, should be in the same style and character as the house. There are many variations of fences, but, in general, use picket or brick in front of a Colonial style house, split rail or post and rail with Early American houses, and post and board or any of the many combinations of board and plywood with a contemporary house. Hedges, of course, go with any architectural style, but they do require clipping several times a year or they lose their bottom leaves and a lot of their ability to screen out the view, noise, and dust.

Foundation planting that has gotten badly out of hand completely hides the graceful lines and detail of this house.

Bricks set on edge to line planting beds are expensive, difficult to keep looking neat, and can be dangerous.

A chain-link fence around the perimeter of the property offers the most security, but is the least attractive unless covered with vines or hedge. Closely planted privet will discourage dogs and cats from digging under it to get in—or out.

Contrary to popular thought, good fences do make good neighbors because they define property lines and keep other people's children and pets out of your yard and garden. An attractive fence is a good background for shrubbery and plants, but do not put up a low picket fence that someone could injure himself on by falling over it.

The smaller the yard and garden, the more carefully it must be designed. Back of the house, away from the noisy street, is where most of us will want to concentrate our time and efforts. There should be a play area away from the driveway where children can be seen from a kitchen window, and there should also be a place for adults to relax in quiet and privacy. If you live on a busy street, the sound of splashing water from a small fountain will help obscure the noise from the traffic and is very relaxing. Small inexpensive motors recirculate the water.

Gardens: Grow your own fresh vegetables, even if there is no space for a separate vegetable garden, by mixing them in with flowers that require the same moisture and type of soil. Edge the beds with plastic or aluminum strips so the lawn mower will go over them, making a nice crisp line (and making mowing much easier). Do not use sawtooth bricks to edge flower beds because children can fall on them and cut themselves, and because they

make cutting the grass near them very difficult (they are also ugly). And those "cute" little round or oval flower beds in the middle of an expanse of lawn look out of place, need a lot of work, and tend to get particularly shabby if not kept in tip-top shape. Concentrate your planting in one or two areas rather than having a little bit here and a little bit there.

Ground cover: Grass requires a lot of attention and a good lawn is expensive, although it will keep down noise, absorb heat rays from the sun, and provide a soft green setting for play and relaxation. You can use no-maintenance ground cover such as ivy, pachysandra, Virginia creeper, running myrtle, or vinca under trees where grass will not grow, and on steep banks where it is difficult to run a lawn mower. It is much easier to care for a terraced hillside than one planted with grass. Terracing makes the hillside usable for vegetable and flower gardens and as a place to walk. Every other terrace or so, provide a bench to sit on and relax so you can really enjoy the garden and the privacy it gives you.

You can use ground covers in combination with islands of grass, brick, slate, or gravel. You can eliminate grass entirely from your garden if you have raised planting beds that spill over with colorful annuals surrounded by walks of brick or slate set in sand. Raised planting beds make it easier for an elderly person to seed and garden; if the beds are properly designed and not too deep, there is no need to kneel or bend to tend them. Raised beds also discourage children and pets from digging in the petunias, and you can isolate bushes, flowers, and vegetables that require different kinds of soil and fertilizer and amounts of water.

The garden should be lit, but with very low wattage—just enough to illuminate a path or any steps, and perhaps to highlight a specimen plant in bloom, such as a rose bush or azalea. Candles in hurricane holders provide a lovely soft light for a garden, and are just as pleasant for the shadows they cast over white snow and green foliage. Arrange lighting so it does not shine into a neighbor's windows, especially if you install bright security lights.

The Driveway

Our automobiles have become such a big part of our lives that they may be considered as extensions of our homes. Therefore they must be treated well. We should be able to get out of them and into our homes as con-

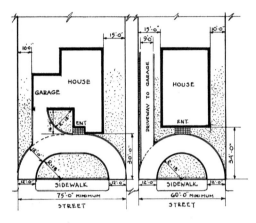

Minimum dimensions of a circular driveway based on a turning radius of nineteen feet for a Chevrolet. A 27-foot radius is required for a #75 Cadillac limousine.

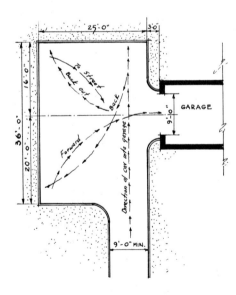

Turning space required for the average American car backing out of a garage.

veniently and safely as possible. Conversely, we should be able to get into our cars easily and maneuver into traffic with the least amount of danger to our families, ourselves, and our neighbors.

A driveway is a place where children like to play, and no matter how much you scold, they will roller skate, ride tricycles, play hopscotch and ball there. Backing out of the garage and parking spaces is inevitable, but the driveway should be designed to keep backing to a minimum. Obviously, if you have to back from the driveway into traffic, you need a new driveway.

The driveway should lead your guests to, and point out, your front entrance, and the parking area beyond should be obvious. Too many driveways ignore a hidden front door and lead straight to the back door and garage. If this is true of your driveway, either the drive or the front door should be changed.

The circular drive: The best solution is usually a circular drive. You need a minimum of 60 feet of footage for the average American car, a minimum width of 12 feet on curves and 9 feet on the straightaway. Parking space will depend on how many cars your family has and how many guests you usually have at one time. (Most zoning ordinances prohibit street parking.) Distances between parked cars should be large enough so that the doors may be opened without chipping the paint of the car in the next space. Allow a minimum width of 9 feet per car for parking.

Connect the drive to the utility area of the house so that a garbage truck and other services can get in and out. In the North, short driveways make snow shoveling easier. If you have your drive plowed out commercially, place trees and evergreens where they will not be broken by snow piled on them. On a hill, try to curve the driveway to slow the descent of your car and to prevent rain or melting snow from freezing into a straight slide to the street.

There should be a crown, or higher level, in the center of the drive so that water drains off on each side. Edge the sides so grass will not grow over the driveway.

Avoid the temptation to construct a rustic arch over the entrance to your driveway—unless you live on a ranch in Texas or Oklahoma—because a delivery van or garbage truck is likely to knock it down. If you want a gate, place it an automobile length in from the street so that when you stop to open it you will be out of a traffic lane. For security when opening the gate at night, there should be a light on one or both sides. If you have only one light, it should be on the left or driver's side.

The material for a driveway can be concrete, blacktop, gravel, or brick. Brick is the most expensive, but by far the most attractive.

Brick: A brick driveway can be laid without mortar in sand. This can easily be done by hand if the drive has been shaped and smoothed properly. Plastic sheets laid in strips under the brick will provide drainage while minimizing the amount of grass and weeds that make their way through.

Blacktop: A blacktop or commercial asphalt driveway will have to be done by a professional paver and is subject to some deterioration. However, children do like it for roller skating and games. Weeds will grow right through it, so it should be edged with plastic or aluminum and weeded at least once a year back to the edging.

Concrete: A concrete driveway requires no maintenance, but oil, dirt, and tire marks will discolor it in places. To keep it from cracking, you may have to provide expansion joints. Good drainage is essential under concrete to keep it from freezing out in winter.

Gravel: Do not use gravel for driveways on steep grades because it tends to wash down and build up at the bottom of the incline. On sharp curves, gravel gets pushed to the side and has to be raked back periodically. New gravel has to be put down every few years. A gravel drive should be edged not only to keep the grass from growing over it, but also to keep the gravel out of the grass. A gravel driveway should have a hardpan, asphalt, or crushed stone base to keep the gravel from mixing with mud in the rainy season and disappearing. With proper drainage and a good base, a gravel drive will not be slippery in icy

weather and your tires will have good traction, but frequent snow plowing will remove a lot of the gravel.

Driveways should only be put down by a reputable contractor, and you should have a plan, specifications with written starting and finishing dates, and a guarantee. Do not let just anyone who knocks at the door and is "working in the neighborhood" sign you up for work, even if he offers a very cheap price.

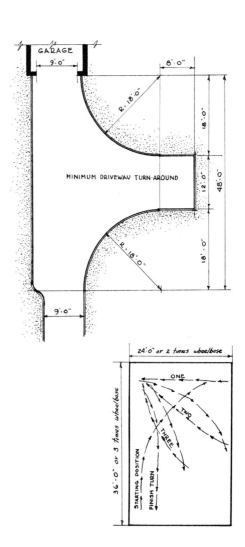

Minimum space required for backing and turning out of a garage or parking space in one turn . . . and in three turns.

Here, a loggia enclosing a courtyard connects the front door to the driveway. Wrought iron gates or a wooden door would provide additional privacy and security.

The Entrance

Your entrance is the introduction to your house and, like all first impressions, it is a very important statement about your home and you. The entrance should be visible from the street or the driveway and should lead to the front door. The front door need not be visible from the street, but the way to get to it should be obvious.

If the entrance is hidden and the driveway does not lead directly past it, perhaps you can design the remodeling so that a new entrance is on the drive, or redesign the drive to go past the present entrance. The entrance to a house does not have to be in front or on the side facing the street; it can be on one side of the house or in the back as long as it is easy to find. It should have a broad covered platform to keep rain and snow away from the front door and off your guests as they wait for you to answer the door.

Exterior stairs (top) are awkward and offer no protection from weather. Facade is improved (below) by a new entrance with interior stairs leading to the main floor, and a hall providing covered access to basement and garage.

Keep stairs and handrails well lighted at night and drain the platform and stairs to the side so melting snow does not freeze on them. A mud scraper and doormat will keep water and dirt from being tracked inside. The minimum depth for an entrance is 4 feet, which allows a screen or storm door to be opened without pushing anyone backwards down the steps.

The steps and pavement to the entrance should be at least 5 feet wide so three people can walk in together easily and the elderly and infirm can be helped to and from their cars when it is icy.

The front door does not have to be directly behind the entrance, but the entrance should point the way to the door. The door may be in a courtyard that is approached through a loggia, or it may be simply a covered walkway from the parking area to the door.

Interior stairs: If your house is on a hill sloping up from the street and requires an exposed stair from the driveway to the front door, you can create a new entrance in the basement, with easy and protected stairs on the interior. Or, if space within the house is tight, it may be better to add a new entrance and stair housed in its own structure. The advantages of the latter are numerous. It will give the exterior a whole new look, and if the

front door led directly into the living room, the new entrance will eliminate that problem. You will also gain a snow- and rain-free entrance, as well as driveway access to the basement areas. This is especially important if you have a recreation room or other activity room in the basement, since children and guests can remove wet coats downstairs instead of in the living room. The structure will cost more but it may provide additional closet space, and interior stairs are not as expensive to construct as exterior stairs because they do not have to be designed to take the weather.

The roof on an entrance should be the same type used on the rest of the house, unless you prefer a flat roof, which can be assimilated into the facade of almost any house. Do not try to protect the front door with a plastic or aluminum awning type of roof. These are very ugly and will cheapen the appearance of your house.

Materials: The materials you use will depend on the design and the materials used elsewhere in the house. Do not change to another material if you can avoid doing so. Wood is the worst choice for exterior floors and stairs, as anyone with an old exposed porch can tell you. Wood requires paint, is slippery when wet, splinters, rots, and curls.

Masonry is best for exterior stairs and floors, brick and stone offering the most secure footing because of their rough texture. Slate can be handsome, but it is slippery when wet and has a tendency to ice up. Concrete is the least expensive and may be painted. However, if it is to be painted, it should have a rougher surface than usual to retain its traction. If it is smoothly finished and painted, it will be slippery when wet.

Entrance Hall

Every house has an entrance hall whether it seems to or not. For years, builders and developers have been omitting the entrance hall from houses, in the hope that this would make the living room look bigger. It may, but if there is no entrance hall, there is no true living room, because then the living room must act also as an entranceway.

An entrance hall keeps drafts, wind, heat, and cold from entering the rooms of the house.

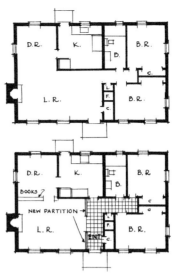

New partitions in the living room (bottom) *create an entrance hall and screen the unwanted view of the bedroom/bathroom hall* (top).

It can also insulate the rooms from street sounds and provide space where people may remove coats, hats, and boots. There should be a closet for wraps and umbrellas in the entrance hall close to the door. A small chest of drawers to hold car keys, sunglasses, and gloves should be against another wall, with a mirror over it for last-minute checks on hair and makeup.

If you do not have an entrance hall, you should add one. Even a small one is better than none at all. If the front door leads into the living room and there is no closet beside it, you can cut off a portion of the room, partition it, and build a closet. True, you will lose space in the living room, but the gain in convenience is worth it. The partitioned entrance hall may actually improve the living room by adding extra wall space. An entrance hall means a quieter house and more privacy.

Designing: When you are designing the entrance hall, there are several things to keep in mind. Avoid views of the kitchen sink, of a bedroom hallway, or a bathroom from the door. These things may seem trivial, but they really are not. If you are to get full value out of the remodeling, you should be sure that every change or addition accomplishes at least two things. For instance, as in the illustration, by simply adding one partition wall and a new door to the kitchen, (1) an entrance hall has been created, (2) the view from the living room down the bedroom hall has been eliminated and the bedrooms will be quieter,

(3) the door from the kitchen to the entrance hall will save steps when the front door must be answered, and (4) bookshelves separating part of the dining room from the living room create a feeling of space around the fireplace. It still may not be the best house in the world, but one small remodeling job has accomplished a lot.

Creating a new entrance may be easier than you think. Analyze the circulation within your house, note how it works with the driveway and the outdoors—in other words, observe your pattern of living.

You will also want to be able to see who is at the door without being seen yourself, but do not place a large expanse of glass next to the door. This will provide very little security, and if the door should slam closed, the glass may be broken. The entrance hall is the logical place for stairs to the second floor or to the basement if there is to be a recreation room there. So perhaps by studying the circulation,

adding only an entrance, and relocating the stairs, you can remodel and upgrade your home.

An entrance hall does not have to be pat and standard. In the house shown, for instance, the entrance was a sort of box stuck on the front. There was room for little more than a chair in the living room, which was used chiefly as a passageway between the bedroom and kitchen. A new entrance porch, set back from the street and not looking at all like a porch, was added. The old entrance was torn down and the space it had occupied, along with an ungainly window, was replaced with a bay window, which opened the living room to the century-old trees outside. A closet was added and the stairs were redesigned. A Franklin stove was placed on a brick hearth. The entrance porch is a marvelous outdoor summer living room, open to the garden and easily accessible from the kitchen. Sliding glass doors close it off from the weather in seconds.

The architectural rendering at right showed in advance how the small house (top left) *would look after the entrance hall and porch were added* (bottom left).

Stairs

Stairs can be an exciting experience in getting from one floor to the next, or they can be dangerous and tiresome. The tread of a stair is the flat part where you step; the rise is the vertical distance between treads. This combination of riser and tread is called the "rise over run." The dimensions of tread and riser should remain constant on every staircase or people will lose their stride and stumble. If stairs are properly designed, the run plus twice the rise should equal 25; or, when the run is multiplied by the rise, the figure should be 75.

Sometimes stairs are made steep in an effort to save floor space, but this makes for a difficult stair, especially if adequate head room is not provided. The minimum clearance from the tread to any floor joist spanning the stair should be 6 feet 8 inches.

Landings should be incorporated into the design of every stair if possible, not only to provide a place to pause for breath on the way up, but also to break your fall if you should stumble on the way down.

Winders, used to save space and shorten the length of the stair, are dangerous and should not be used. You should not have a window on a landing or at the bottom of a run of stairs because if someone should trip and fall, they may go through the glass.

Most stairs are 3 feet wide, but this is merely convention. If you habitually help someone up and down, a 4-foot width is better. Stairs can be as narrow as 2 feet if the narrow width allows you to make the rise over run more leisurely and gives you wider landings, but keep in mind that the wider a stair is, the easier it will be to move furniture up and down. Basement stairs should have a 3-foot landing on the basement side of the stairs if the door to the basement opens onto the stair.

Circular stairs can save a lot of space, their cost is not prohibitive, and they are not difficult to assemble, but they should be used carefully and only as a second means of getting up or down. Small children, the elderly, and some others cannot negotiate them (I have had to carry an otherwise fearless 140-lb. German shepherd down one of them).

Stairs should be lighted. Use a three-way switch that works at top, bottom, and on every landing. Carpet with underpadding will make all stairs quieter and safer.

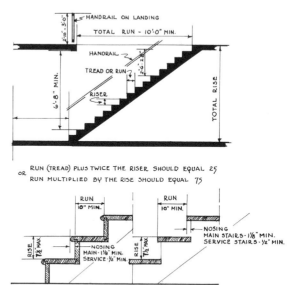

Elements of closed and open stairs.

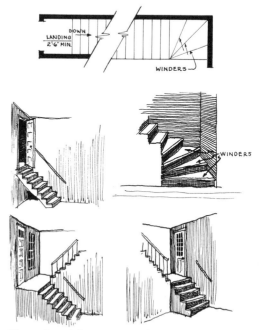

Examples of dangerous stairways.

Living Room

Whether you remodel your present living room or add a new one will depend on the circulation within your house and how you want to use the new room. Make sure first that you really want and need a new living room. Too many living rooms are not for living; they are simply rooms housing a lot of expensive furniture, carpeting, drapes, and a fireplace that is never lit because the study or the family room is much more comfortable. This type of living room has been relegated to the status of the front parlor of our grandmothers' day—it is used only on special occasions.

The other extreme is the living room that is overused because it is a connecting corridor between the dining room, kitchen, bedrooms, bathroom, and the front and back doors. This type of living room is inevitably at the front of the house, facing the street, and lacks quiet and privacy. Instead of overlooking the lovely garden in back of the house, the view is of the neighbors across the street. Some living rooms are not only noisy and public from the outside, but also from the inside. When everyone uses the living room for everything, it is hard to keep clean and is in a constant state of confusion and disarray.

What you can do with your living room depends on its size, whether or not the windows can be changed to give you privacy from the street, and whether or not there is enough space to reorganize the circulation with partitions. After you make all these changes, will the living room be in the best location for your house? In most cases, the larger the room, the easier it is to make it into usable space, but size alone does not determine if a room will function well or badly. Let us look at several common living rooms to see what can be done with them.

A: In living room A, the fireplace is opposite the entrance to the room, where people will be drawn to it. There is a wall space large enough for a sofa and end tables opposite a bay window overlooking the garden, while smaller windows on the front of the house give privacy from the street. There is even enough wall space for a grand piano, and since it is a

dead-end living room, it can be furnished easily although conventionally.

B: Living room B is difficult to furnish easily or conventionally. The fireplace blocks the view of the garden, the bay window faces the street, it is hard to find furnishings that are at home in front of sliding glass doors. A talented designer could make the room look re-

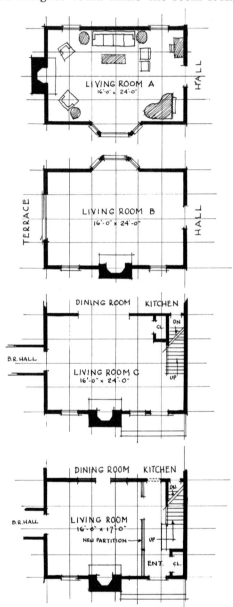

Large living rooms can be easy or difficult to furnish and use depending on the location and design of doors and windows. Here are three living room plans, and (bottom) a remodeling of plan C.

spectable, even handsome, but it would never work as well as plan A. There is no place to put anything where it will not be in front of something else. It is difficult to achieve a balance with this kind of a room.

C: Plan C is a situation many people are confronted with. It is not entirely hopeless. The entrance to the house is in the living room, the windows face the street, and all are much too close to the fireplace for safety from sparks when the door is opened and the draft changes. The window beside the front door allows strangers to look through the living room into the dining room, the closet is in a poor location, there is a view down the bedroom hall from just about everywhere, and there is no way to place furniture except in a Girl Scout circle around the fireplace.

One solution would be to place the closet in a better location and run a hall to the kitchen. The partition does not need to be ceiling height (if it were, the room might be dark and gloomy with all the light and ventilation concentrated to the right of the fireplace), and after it passes the edge of the new closet, it could become open bookshelves. The bedroom hallway will have to be closed off with a door—not the best solution, but the only one available.

D: Plan D is a common problem living room in a typical house built in the 1940s, when they were selling for under $4,000, including the lot. When a living room is hopeless, you might as well admit it, and this one is by today's standards. The only solution is to add a new living room. In doing so, you can gain more than just additional space because you can turn the old living room into a family room that is in the center of the house where it can be used by everyone all the time. Since there is an entrance hall and laundry, the clothes do not have to be carted to the basement and back for washing. The kitchen has been enlarged and dining space has been set aside in it for breakfast. For more formal dinners, the family room could be used. Because of zoning restrictions, however, you may not be able to build an addition to the side of your house. Then your only solution would be to build the new living room in the backyard.

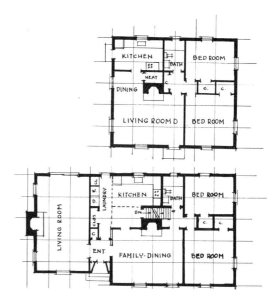

A typical 1940 house with a difficult living room (top) *remodeled with an addition to one side* (bottom).

E: The Plan E living room provides an entrance on the driveway that connects the new living room to the rest of the house, creating an enclosed courtyard which can be entered from the kitchen. For complete privacy, the courtyard could be walled. If that seems too confining, an 8-foot-high wall could be run from the far living room wall to the bedroom.

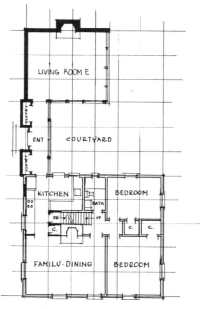

The same 1940 house, with an addition at the back and the entrance off the driveway.

Dining Room

Dining rooms are not used much anymore, even by people with big families, because serving in the kitchen or family room is so much easier. People who entertain a lot usually do so outdoors in the summer, or serve a buffet in the family room in the winter. When there are just a few people living at home, it can be pleasant to simply take a tray to the fireplace and the television.

Many development houses advertise dining rooms that are only an alcove off the living room, seating six or less, with no space left over for buffets or sideboards. The living room is not the best place for a dining table and chairs. It is usually a long walk from the kitchen, which makes serving a chore, and the table tends to be used for other activities such as games, homework, and a place to put mail and magazines or build model airplanes. Obviously, you do need dining space somewhere, whether it is in a room of its own or in another room.

Planning: If you think you can get all the members of your family together in one room at a given hour every day over a period of years, and you want a dining room, make sure it is of sufficient size to hold a table that will seat everyone. A rule of thumb is two seatings per bedroom, plus two additional seatings for every three people living in the house. If you have a three-bedroom house, allowing 2 feet per person at the table, you would need a dining room with a minimum width of 8 feet 9 inches and length of 12 feet to accommodate a table 2 feet 9 inches wide. Note this minimum-sized room does not allow for any other furniture except dining table and chairs.

Chairs should have a clearance of 3 feet between the table and the wall or another piece of furniture. When you are designing the room, begin with the width of the table, plus 3 feet clearance for the chairs, and add the width of any other furniture you are going to be using to determine the size you need.

Round tables are preferred by many people as more convivial than rectangular tables. They can be used to much better advantage if they are large. For instance, four people can sit at a table 3 feet in diameter, but there would be no room on the table for serving plates, so you would have to be able to reach a sideboard or serving cart.

The kitchen should be separated from the dining room by a swinging door placed at the end of the room. The hostess always sits facing the door to the kitchen so that as it is opened and closed, the guests do not have a view of the possible chaos left behind in the kitchen.

Arrange the dining room so it cannot be viewed from the front door. Do not have large windows overlooking the street in your dining

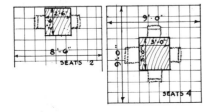

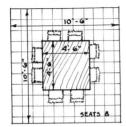

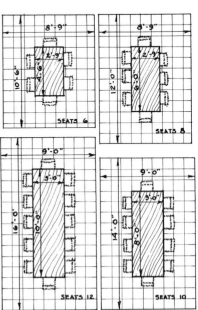

NOTE : EACH SQUARE EQUALS ONE SQUARE FOOT

Floor space required for proper clearance in breakfast and dining rooms with rectangular and square tables.

room, or you will be on display all through dinner unless you draw the drapes. Avoid placing the dining room next to a bathroom, and do not allow a view down a bedroom hallway from the table.

Although a carpeted floor gives you a warmer, quieter dining room, you may find yourself using the room less to avoid crumbs and spills. Carpet or a rug will wear under the chairs, and even sturdy chairs will feel the strain of being pulled up and pushed away from the table. Hard-surface floors, with the possible exception of wood, are easy to care for (spills may be wiped up easily), but they are not as quiet as carpet and chair legs will leave impressions on them. Wood can be lovely, but to keep it that way requires almost constant effort. For good looks, easy care, and convenience, use solid vinyl tile.

Lighting: Very important in the dining area, lighting can make food look better, taste better, and help you relax and enjoy your meal. Restaurants have lighting down to a science. Cafeterias light their steam tables with pink lights to make meats and vegetables more appetizing but, like quick snack bars, light their dining tables brightly so customers will eat quickly and leave. The brighter the light, the faster you eat.

Wall lights above a buffet cast a gentle glow over the room, and a pin-spot down light will illuminate only the surface of the table.

These can be controlled with inexpensive rheostats, and you can augment them with candles, so the simplest dinner becomes a pleasant experience.

Have extra convenience outlets beside, but not behind, a buffet for warming trays and electric coffeemakers. Put a convenience outlet under the table if you want to have small appliances such as a toaster, waffle iron, or electric coffeepot beside you on the table.

To double the use of your dining room, make it a semi-library, with a fireplace on one end, a wall lined with books, and several comfortable lounge chairs. A window seat is also an excellent addition to a dining room as a quiet and comfortable place to retreat to and read. Who can resist having dinner or reading in front of a cozy fire, which can also be used to heat the room on cold afternoons and evenings?

When you entertain, a separate dining room does have the advantage of allowing you to leave the room with your guests, close the door, and forget about cleaning up until the guests have gone. Sitting down all together for a meal in a dining room will also let you supervise your children's diet more readily, and teach them the table manners that will be important to them later in life and that so few young people have.

A round table, and the combining of modern architecture with antique furniture, makes this small dining room look and feel spacious.

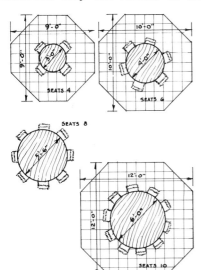

Floor space required for clearance in rooms using round dining tables.

Family Room

If the living room of your house has become overcrowded with books, magazines, records and record player, television, piano, a permanently set up folding card table for games and puzzles, the baby's playpen, and one of your children's friends sleeping on the sofa overnight, you need either a new living room or a family room.

A family room does not have to be next to or part of the kitchen, but if you have small children who need watching and youngsters who are constantly hungry, the closer to the kitchen the family room is, the more it will be used. If you have a dining room that is not being used, you might consider making it into a family room and turning the living room back into a living room again. The wall, or part of it, between the kitchen and family room can be removed and counter space created on both sides. This will also afford you a view of the room so you can supervise the children.

You may not have a dining room to convert, or, since the family room is usually the noisiest room in the house, you may want to make a living room now fronting a busy street into the family room, and build a new living room at the back of the house overlooking the garden where it will be more private and quiet. If the family room is placed at the front of the house, it will act as a buffer between the noisy street and the other rooms.

A garage that is near the kitchen may be made into an excellent family room. Perhaps all you will have to do is remove the wall between, insulate and finish the garage walls and ceiling, and replace the garage door with a sliding glass door.

Planning: A family room should be more than just a repository for old furniture that you do not want to use anywhere else. The same thought and care in design and planning should go into it as into any other important room. Exposure should be considered. The room should get sunlight during the winter, not only to help heat it, but also to make it more cheerful. Since you will want to keep sunlight out in summer for the sake of coolness, install overhangs or plant large trees to shade the windows.

A room added to the north side of a one-story house will be flooded with sunlight in the winter if you roof the family room addition with a shed roof containing a clerestory window all along its length. Provide an overhang and make the windows operable for creating a cooling breeze through the room in summer.

A fireplace is a welcome inclusion in almost any room, but particularly in a family room because it will get the most use there. If a masonry fireplace is too expensive or inconvenient, a Franklin stove will take the chill and the gloom off the room in a matter of minutes. The flues really do get very warm, so do not place them close to glass or it is apt to get broken from the rapid rise in heat. A fireplace (constructed or prefabricated) or a Franklin stove will make some extra dirt, but the saving on fuel and the glow of the fire are well worth it. The materials used in a family room should be as dirt- and child-proof as possible.

Frank Russell

A two-car garage remodeled into a bright and pleasant family room.

Try to plan your family room so that you can include a porch off it. In the summer, you can move a table and other furniture out there, thus doubling the size and use of the room. You can still get sunlight into the family room by including a large skylight over the doors to the porch, and you can move some of your favorite plants indoors during the winter months. Geraniums and orange trees, for instance, will last for years this way.

Plan lots of storage space in the form of open shelves for books and games that are used often, and closed cabinets for things that are only used occasionally. A big toy box that doubles as a coffee table and footstool can be built from materials left over from the construction of the room.

If the kitchen is open to the family room, you can separate the two functions with a wide counter top. That way you will not have to worry about falling over toys and you will still be able to keep an eye on things. The counter should be at least 3 feet wide, with doors on the kitchen and family room side so you can get to the storage area from each room. You can use it as a serving counter, buffet, or snack bar; you may even cook on it with an electric skillet or broiler. If the counter also houses the washer and dryer on the family room side, the top would be good for sorting clothes.

Design the furniture placement and arrange the most convenient electric outlets. Usually it is a mistake to hang a ceiling fixture over a dining table, because as your children grow, the way the room is used will change and the fixture could be a nuisance.

Radiant heating in the floor will warm the baby's playpen and any small children playing on the floor. The flooring material could be tile, brick, wood planks, or indoor-outdoor carpet. Do not use the standard hardwood flooring which requires so much maintenance. Keep all the materials simple, rough, and sturdy so you can relax and enjoy the room along with the rest of your family.

What had been a usual living room with picture window is remodeled and extended into a family room separated from the porch by a huge skylight, which allows orange trees and geraniums to bloom all winter.

Kitchen

The kitchen is undoubtedly the most expensive room in the house. It is also the most important because it is used constantly. Your house and family life revolves around the kitchen, so it must be convenient and adaptable. A frustrating kitchen means an irritating day. It should be comfortable and pleasant to work in and easy to clean; it should give you a lift in the morning and not tire you at night; and it should be light, bright, airy, and beautiful. That is a lot for one room to live up to, but it can be done.

Your kind of kitchen: No two women (or men, for that matter) run a kitchen the same way. Some ladies would not dream of entering the cook's domain; some begin their day

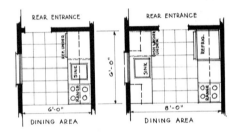

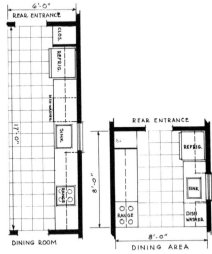

Medium-sized one-wall and galley kitchens. Over 20 feet in length, a one-wall kitchen becomes inefficient.

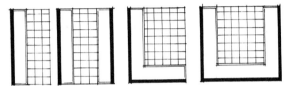

One-wall, galley, L-, and U-shaped kitchens.

by cooking breakfast in their kitchens and never leave them all day. Your kitchen is as personal as your toothbrush. Some people want everyone out of the kitchen when they cook, and there are other families where everybody is invited into the act. The first style means a closed kitchen; the second, an open kitchen.

A closed kitchen requires a tight plan, with steps between refrigerator, sink, and range minimized and just the right amount of counter space between. It does *not* mean a kitchen that is isolated, where the housewife is walled off from the family and guests.

An open kitchen is one that has more space between appliances so that several people can work and move around without bumping into each other. There may be a big kitchen table in the middle of the room and a baby's high chair in the corner.

Whether you remodel your kitchen in its present location, move it to another part of the house, or build it in a new addition de-

pends on your house and the way you want to work in your kitchen.

The least expensive way to remodel your kitchen is to leave everything pretty much in its present location—but this is not remodeling the kitchen to make it better, it is just changing it (though that may be all it needs). Chances are, though, if your kitchen is old and inconvenient, more than a change is required.

Moving the sink to get it under a window and reshuffling the appliances in the present space for a better work pattern are neither complicated nor expensive changes. What is a problem is the kind of arrangement where each appliance stands alone in isolated splendor without connecting counter tops because every other foot of wall space is taken up by doors, windows, and openings to other rooms. If your kitchen has a back door, a door to the basement, garage, dining room, and hall, a back stair to the second floor, and several windows, using the existing space will require closing some of these openings—unless it is

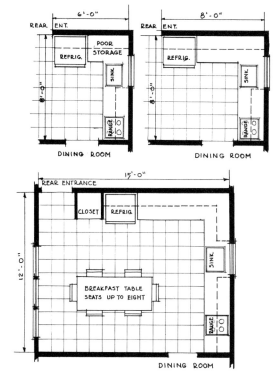

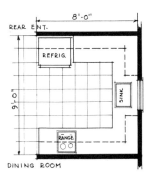

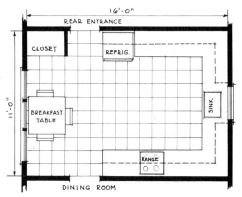

Undersized L-shaped kitchen (top left) does not provide good under-countertop storage. Minimum 8-foot-square kitchen (top middle) is better, and allows space for breakfast table opposite refrigerator. A large L-shaped kitchen (bottom) is efficient and provides ample space for table.

Minimum-sized (8 by 9 feet) U-shaped kitchen is easiest to work in and the most efficient, but even a larger size does not provide the spaciousness of the L-shaped kitchen.

an exceptionally large room and you can lump everything together in one big island in the middle and work from four sides. In a small room, the openings will have to be moved to new locations or eliminated entirely. This can usually be done, but depending on how much they are used and how useful they really are.

Maybe you can spread out into the dining room, or perhaps you can enclose the porch and use that space too. Another possibility is to leave the room as it is and use it as a breakfast room, while building an entirely new kitchen.

An all-new kitchen in a new addition is the most expensive remodeling, because it requires a structure, new plumbing, electricity, heating, fixtures, cabinets, and, most likely, a building permit—which means increased property taxes. Think about the first two possibilities, and only after they have been considered and discarded, plan the new addition..

Kitchen designs: Basically, there are only four kitchen designs and they all use the same principles of storing (refrigerator and cabi-

nets), cleaning (sink), cooking (range), and serving (table). The four designs are the one-wall kitchen, the galley or parallel kitchen, the L-shaped kitchen, and the U-shaped kitchen. There is also the island kitchen in which everything, perhaps excluding the refrigerator, is grouped together and you can work on three or four sides of it.

Any one of these designs may be a closed or open kitchen—just as any one of them may be inconvenient and difficult to work in, depending on the designer. Success is a matter of size and the placement of appliances.

The one-wall kitchen is for a small space. There is not very much base cabinet storage, although perhaps the wall cabinets can make up for the lack. If a one-wall kitchen is designed to run too long, you will have to do a lot of walking back and forth when preparing meals. The one-wall kitchen is a good solution if a small pantry can be placed at one end, or if it can be designed without a wall and window separating it from the family room or dining room.

Handsome and efficient, this minimum-sized U-shaped kitchen is dramatically lighted with a skylight.

The galley kitchen is an expanded one-wall kitchen, with the appliances against one or both walls. The minimum width is 8 feet. The galley may also be used to separate the kitchen from the family room or dining room, and may include a pantry or a washer and dryer at one end.

The L-shaped kitchen is favored by many people because half the area is available for a breakfast table. Every kitchen should have room for a small table, if only for feeding the baby or relaxing with a cup of coffee. A minimum amount of space is required for either a dishwasher beside the sink or for space between the counter and the refrigerator. A small corner base cabinet is very poor storage space.

The U-shaped kitchen is usually preferred for its simplicity, maximum storage in the least amount of space, and minimum number of steps required to prepare a meal. However, it will not be convenient if the space in the center is large enough for a table and chairs

because then you will constantly have to walk around these obstacles.

Cabinets: Wall cabinets are usually 12 inches deep and mounted 18 inches over base cabinets, 30 inches over the range. In remodeling, they are usually not built to the ceiling because the ceilings in older houses tend to be uneven. Thus you will have a lot of wasted space, so if you can build your own cabinets or have them made on the job by a carpenter, take them almost to the ceiling and put a small molding around to hide any cracks. Build them onto the wall without backs so there will be no place for insects to hide. Both base and wall cabinets can be built with adjustable metal shelves so that no dust or dirt collects in them. Doors are a simple matter of hinged plywood. Catches are either friction or magnetic, magnetic being better because it is quiet and does not need the precise fit a friction catch does.

You can, of course, buy ready-made wood and metal cabinets, but they are very expensive. Metal cabinets may rust, are noisy, and, like wood cabinets, come with backs on them which some people consider a disadvantange, especially in an older home.

If you do have to buy cabinets, get only the simplest. Broom closets, for instance, are not used any more because people do not sweep, they vacuum the kitchen floor. Bread drawers are no longer used (at least, not for bread) because bread keeps better in the refrigerator.

Lighting: The most important light in the kitchen is the one over the sink. If you can have only one fixture in your kitchen, put it there and not in the center of the room where it will throw everything into shadow.

Counter lights under the wall cabinets give excellent illumination where and when you need it. They are very slim, and when turned off, you do not see them.

You can get desirable east light in your kitchen by installing a skylight or dormer if there is a one-story room blocking the east wall. If the kitchen is on the north side of the house, you could add a bay window over the sink. You might also get sunlight by slanting the wall and putting in a window that faces east.

Bath

Deciding whether you want to remodel an existing bath or add a new one is not difficult. You already know, because you know the size of your family and the inconveniences you presently put up with, the nature of the problem and the best solution.

The most difficult bathroom to remodel is the minimum-sized 5-by-7-foot bathroom where the bathtub is against the outside wall and the toilet and lavatory are tightly jammed together on the wet wall.

Additional space may be gained in the bathroom with a minimum of construction and plumbing extensions by cantilevering the bathroom over the foundation. This would give you a larger, safer bathroom that is easier to clean.

Locating a second bath: If your house has only one bath, the most important consideration in building a second is the location. If you can back a new bath up to an existing wet wall of another bath or a kitchen, you will save on the plumbing—if the pipes can handle the increased load. If you do not want to take the space from a room, you may be able to remodel the existing bath into a large compartmented bathroom which could function as two.

A lot will depend on how the bath is to be used. If it is to be a half-bath (a lavatory and toilet, no bathtub or shower) for guests, place it near the entrance off the front hall, or off the study if that room doubles as a guest room. If the second bath is being added for the use of the entire family, it should be placed off the bedroom hallway. If the bath is to be for the exclusive use of the owner, it can be located off the master bedroom. If it is being built as part of a bedroom addition, provide adequate space as the addition is being built.

Plan for safety: The smaller the bathroom, the more certain you must be that it is safe. Do not put a window over the tub or anywhere else where someone could slip and fall against it. Avoid sharp angles and spaces that are too small to get at to clean easily. If you can have both a tub and a shower stall, put both in because tubs are not really designed for standing. Both should have grab bars firmly anchored to studs and should be able to support your weight. Do not make the bathroom so small and cramped that you cannot faint in it without hitting a half-dozen sharp angles. (When people feel ill, the first place they run is to the bathroom.)

Glass towel bars, shelves, and accessories should never be used in a bathroom. Bathroom dividers and shower stalls should be of unbreakable plastic.

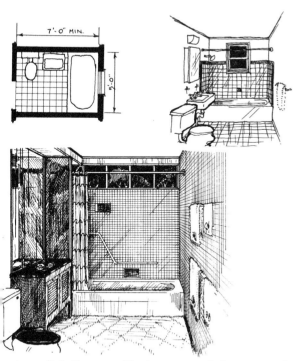

A small bathroom with dangerous window over tub (top) can be remodeled with new fixtures and a high ribbon for light and safety (bottom).

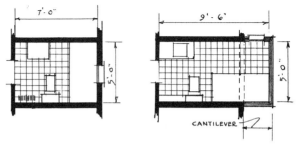

An old-style bathroom (left) can be enlarged by cantilevering. Window can be moved from over tub and plumbing need not be changed or replaced.

Toilets: Fixtures can influence the design and location of the bathroom. There are basically four types of toilets from which to choose, though you may be restricted to what is available in your area.

The wash-down toilet is the cheapest. It has a round bowl, a front drain, and a low water level. It needs a lot of scrubbing, makes a lot of noise, and is apt to overflow.

The reverse-trap and siphon-jet toilets are of the same type, though a step above the wash-down model. They usually function a lot better.

The siphon-vortex toilet is the most sanitary; it is also the most expensive. It cleans itself with a minimum of noise and upkeep.

There are also silent-flush, wall-hung, and corner toilets, which allow you some freedom with the design and placement of the bathroom. The silent-flush toilet is not all that silent, but if the bathroom is next to a dining room or against a wall where quiet is desired, it will keep the noise of rushing water to a minimum.

Wall-hung toilets have clear space under them, thus eliminating cleaning around the base. Since they are mounted on the wall, they can be used over concrete floors in a converted garage or basement. They require 2-by-6 studs and extra bracing in the wall to support them.

Corner toilets allow you to place the fixture in a smaller space (if a corner is available). This can be an advantage if you are making an oversized closet into a guest toilet or powder room.

Bathtubs: Bathtubs have taken on all shapes and shades of color with the introduction of plastic and fiberglass. The standard rectangular bathtub is 5 feet long and 2 feet 6 inches wide. It may be ordered in sizes from 2 feet 4 inches wide to 7 feet long, and is made of enameled cast iron or steel. Cast iron is better, but weighs about 365 pounds, so if you are placing a tub where the weight of tub, water, and bather could cause a problem, choose the lighter, 140-pound steel tub.

Metal tubs also come in square, round, and sunken models. Avoid using the sunken type in an average bathroom. In an old bathroom, the joists must be cut to receive the tub, but if you are adding a new bath, the placement is critical because they are easy to fall into or trip over. Never put a sunken tub where you have to walk past it to another part of the bathroom. It could be a disaster in a typical 5-by-8 foot bathroom.

Square tubs come in various sizes from 3½ feet to more than 4 feet, and in some cases are a great help in constructing a better bathroom in a small space. They are especially good for the elderly and for children because they have a small ledge that can be used as a seat. A square tub is difficult, if not impossible, to clean the traditional way. The only way to clean one is to get into it.

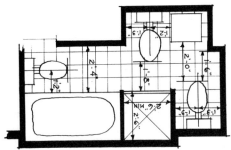

Minimum clearances for bathroom fixtures. For mobility and cleaning ease, leave more room if possible. Special fixture sizes can be ordered for unusual conditions.

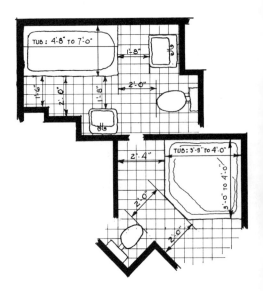

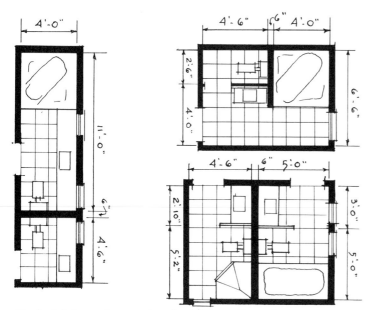

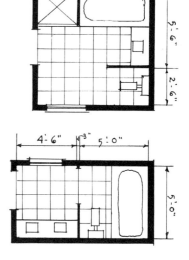

*Typical fixture placement and minimum dimensions
for double and compartmented bathrooms.*

A round tub is deep and is for soaking in the Japanese manner. It would probably not be useful as the only bathtub in the house.

Basins: Lavatory bowls come in a wide assortment of sizes, shapes, styles, and materials. Besides the standard wall basin, which has been around for years, there are many new designs, from corner models to strange shapes imported from Europe. Keep in mind that any basin should be installed so as to be capable of supporting your weight if you lean on it. Cost varies from cheap to very expensive. None is as good or offers the attractiveness and storage that a vanity type lavatory does.

Vanities clearly have the edge whether you have a small space or a whole wall to accommodate them. The best, and the most expensive vanity, is one piece of plastic molded with a bowl and backsplash. It is easy to install and to clean. But there are many kinds of plastic. Some are not as stain-resistant as others, some burst into flame if touched with a match, some permit repair of scratches and stains while others do not, and some may crack and become useless, so do not buy blindly. The chief disadvantage to all of them is that since standard fittings must be placed too close to the edge of the bowl, water is constantly getting on the top and your knuckles will hit the wall of the bowl when you try to wash your hands.

Other bowls are self-rimming and can be set on a tile or formica counter top. The least expensive are those rimmed with aluminum, but they are also the least attractive and the least sanitary. Too, after years of cleaning, the aluminum can become razor sharp.

Tile: Finishing materials in the bathroom should be moistureproof. Ceramic tile walls are a favorite. The new mastics and grouts hold tile well and are so easy to work with that you can tile the bathroom walls in several days yourself. If the wall surface around the tub or shower is to be tiled, it will first have to be covered with waterproof dry wall, plywood, or hardboard so the tile will hold.

Lighting: Bathroom lighting can vary from the glamorous to the sadistic. One small fixture over the mirror above the lavatory is really not sufficient to shave by, and two fluorescent tubes, one on each side of the mirror, will give you a deathly pallor. If you put in a luminous ceiling of dropped panels, you will need additional light on each side of the mirror for shaving. An incandescent light on each side of the mirror, a little lower than eye level, is best for shaving and for applying makeup. If the bathroom is compartmented, additional fixtures will be required.

Bedroom

The trouble with most bedrooms is that they are too small; they can be used only for sleeping. This is, of course, very important, but it is a waste if a room is used only at night. Often, with the addition of just a few more feet, the use of the room could be doubled.

Windows: Many bedrooms may be large enough but, because of the poor placement of windows, flexibility of furniture arrangement is lost. Many small bedrooms can be improved simply by changing the location of the windows. High windows permit a bit more flexibility (which is why builders use them so extensively), and in a crowded neighborhood they can increase privacy, but beds should not be placed under them because of the drafts they create. High windows over a bed are also hard to open, close, clean, and curtain, and if it rains during the night the bed can become soaked.

High windows in a child's room or in an elderly person's room can be disastrous in case of a fire. Often they cannot get out and no one will be able to see them from the outside and help them. If all your bedrooms have only high windows, put in at least one new window that is close enough to the floor so a toddler can reach the sill and be seen in case of emergency.

The ideal location for beds is on an inside wall where there are no drafts, cold walls, or noises penetrating from the outside. If the beds must be placed on an outside wall, never place them under a window. And leave enough space between the edge of the bed and a window so the night stand is also not in front of the window. A breeze coming in could blow curtains against a lamp and knock it to the floor.

Small bedrooms look larger when a bay window is added. Even if quite small, it will open up the room and provide space for a chair and table or a window seat with a desk in front of it for study and reading.

Bedrooms can be enlarged without building expensive footings and foundation walls by cantilevering the walls over the existing foundation. Two or three feet may be added to a room this way. Since you do not really need that much head room everywhere in a room, the ceiling joists can be extended along with the floor joists and much of the old wall can be reused. If you need more wall space or a better location for the beds on a new wall, relocate the windows to the new side walls, where you can gain some additional privacy and excellent cross ventilation.

Locating a new bedroom: If you are going to add a new bedroom, study the location and exposure. Bedrooms on the north stay the coolest in summer, the coldest in winter. The opposite is true of bedrooms on the west,

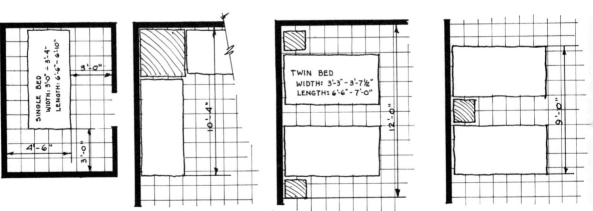

Minimum clearances for single and twin beds in the average bedroom.

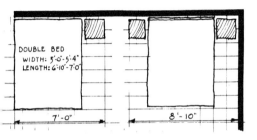

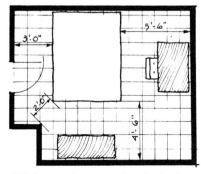

DOUBLE BED
WIDTH: 5'-0"-5'-4"
LENGTH: 6'-10"-7'-0"

Minimum clearances for double beds and furniture placement.

where overhangs cannot protect them from the setting sun. A west bedroom is not good for children who have to go to bed early because of the heat in summer and because the bedroom will stay light the longest.

Most people prefer east light in their bedrooms, because it is cheerful to wake with the sunlight streaming in. East bedrooms are warm in the winter, but not that hot in the summer because of the cool morning air (and perhaps shade from nearby trees).

Bedrooms on the south are excellent for people who are bedridden because the hot summer sun can be kept out with overhangs and the warm winter sun will buoy their spirits.

Most children do not mind a bedroom facing a noisy street, but adults usually prefer a quiet bedroom on the garden side of the house. Also consider the location of your neighbor's garage and driveway. Your working schedules could be so different that his comings and goings might disturb you. (He could also have a wood-working shop in his garage, or a son with a motorcycle.)

Outside noises can often be blocked by a fence or some dense shrubbery along the lot line. Another suggestion is to put a closet along the noisy wall on the inside. The insulation in the wall and the clothing in the closet will absorb most of the noise.

When adding a master bedroom, make it large enough so that it can also be used as a sitting room. Just a few feet will give you enough room to add a desk and several easy chairs so you can use the room to relax, work, or read in, away from the activity in the living room or family room. A small fireplace is not that expensive a luxury in a bedroom that doubles as a retreat.

Children like their privacy, too, and would rather have the smallest room in the house than share the largest. If you are cramped for bedrooms, you could consider dividing the largest bedroom into two rooms and adding a new master bedroom, bath, and dressing room to another part of the house. Another solution might be small dormitory bedrooms arranged around a larger study and play area. The rooms could be furnished with bunks for the youngsters' overnight guests and a small work and storage area of open shelves for their personal belongings and private papers.

We do spend a lot of our lives sleeping, but the best bed in the world is not going to make us more comfortable if the bedroom is not an attractive, pleasant place to relax in and an exciting atmosphere to wake to.

Frank Russell

Well designed, this remodeled master bedroom with a king-sized bed allows ample seating space around the fireplace.

Separate Apartment

If you have an older relative who is thinking of moving in with you, there are certain things to consider when adding or remodeling a room for this purpose. Just a bedroom is usually not enough.

People who have had their own homes or apartments for years have collected small treasures and have taken up hobbies they should be able to pursue. They will also have developed habits and hours that are completely different from your family's. They may want their own beds or furniture in their rooms—not that yours are not good enough, they are just used to their own. They may be unhappy with your rising and dining hours and will feel alienated if made to conform to them. They will want to be with you and your family some of the time, but they will also need privacy and a place to be alone.

Separate facilities: A large room or small apartment on the first floor with a separate entrance and bathroom is the ideal solution. Being on the first floor will eliminate climbing stairs, and a private entrance will let them and their guests come and go as they please.

A separate bathroom is essential, not only for their convenience, but for your own and your family's as well. Older people may have to get up several times during the night, which could disturb light sleepers or someone overly concerned about their well-being. A separate bathroom permits them to keep their medicines separate from the family's and instantly available when they need them.

A small kitchen unit consisting of a combination sink, a two- or three-burner range, and an undercounter refrigerator will enable them to make their own breakfast when they want it and have friends to dinner without interfering with your dinner hours.

The location of the apartment is of particular importance. The apartment should get sunlight most of the day. There should be a view of the garden and the children's play area, but a view capable of being closed off when an older person is not baby sitting and wants to shut out the noise of active children or a neighborhood barbecue. A view of the

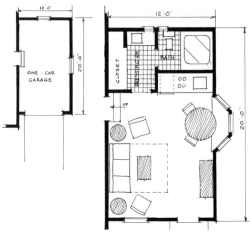

A single-car garage remodeled into a studio apartment. Single-unit kitchens, containing a refrigerator, sink, and range, are available in widths as small as 4 feet.

street is essential. When people are not that active, they enjoy the activities of others and like to watch who is coming and going.

Garage into apartment: Remodeling an attached garage into an apartment is an excellent way to provide practical and attractive, separate but equal, living quarters for relatives. It is fairly simple, quick, and inexpensive if the garage is in good condition. Since the garage is attached to the house, you can extend the heating and electricity into the new area. Plumbing is simplified if the kitchen is close at hand.

Garage floors are several steps below the house floor, but you will want to bring the apartment floor up to the house floor level. The space underneath can be used to run pipes and heating ducts through the basement wall of the house to the far side of the garage wall to provide perimeter heating.

A two-car garage, of course, gives you a lot more space to work with, but even a one-car garage can add valuable space to the interior of your house. The driveway will have to be relocated to a certain extent because you will not want it to disappear under a wall. The part of the drive directly in front of the new wall should be removed for a distance of at least 5 feet to provide space for foundation planting, unless you want to use the driveway as the base for a raised planter along that side.

The Garage

If you are going to add a garage to your house, do it so that you end up with more than just a place to park the car. You can include a workshop, potting shed, or greenhouse to one side, and extra storage either off the body of the garage or in an attic over the garage for very little more than the cost of the garage itself. You can situate the garage so that it encloses a private courtyard off the kitchen or dining room. You could create a new entrance with a loggia to the front door for very little additional money, especially if you can do the work yourself. For a more expansive project, you might build a studio apartment or guest room over the new garage.

You should use the same type of building materials for the garage, as used on the house, though they do not have to match exactly. The style and color are most important. If the roof line is not properly designed and integrated with the house, a garage addition will ruin the facade, especially if the house is traditional and the garage modern.

Aesthetics: Try not to have the garage doors facing the street. They have an empty look when open and the interior of a garage —an easy and automatic space for storing everything from bicycles to unused suitcases— can give the best-designed facade a distressing appearance. Garage doors also have a commercial look and can make your house look more like a filling station or a firehouse than a home. By placing the doors away from the street, you can increase the apparent size of the house and give it more character than it had before.

Connecting the garage to the house with a breezeway is all right if it also separates the street from a rear terrace or garden. Too often, however, the breezeway will collect the bicycles and garden tools that will not fit in the garage, which considerably lessen its appeal as an entrance, and may pose hazards. A breezeway usually does not give much protection from the elements—it is just what it says it is—and snow and rain will blow through when you need protection the most.

Size: How large a garage you need will

Top to bottom: extra bedrooms or an apartment over a garage; small potting shed or shop added to a garage; a garage added to create a private courtyard; a loggia on one side of a garage providing a covered walk from driveway to door.

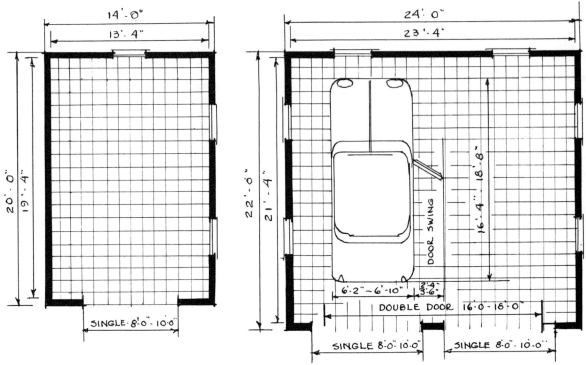

The minimum-sized single-car garage is 12 by 20 feet, but a 14-foot width is advisable for ease getting in and out of the car. A 24-foot width should be allowed for a two-car garage, so that car doors do not chip paint off the neighboring automobile. A depth of 22 feet allows the trunk to be loaded or unloaded conveniently with the garage doors closed.

depend on the number of cars to be parked there. The average American car is about 18 feet long and about 6 feet 8 inches wide. The minimum interior width for a garage is 11 feet 6 inches, but something approaching 14 feet is better. Minimum interior width for a two-car garage is 21 feet 6 inches, although 24 feet allows you to open the doors without scraping or chipping the paint from the next car (the extra few feet do not cost that much more). The minimum length is 20 feet, but 22 to 24 feet is better if you want to be able to load or unload the trunk inside the garage without having to open the garage doors.

Always include a second garage door—not only as a safety measure, but also for convenience' sake in case you want to get something out of the garage and do not want to open the big overhead door.

The floor of the garage should be concrete, sloped to the door to drain. You could also include a floor drain and a hose bib in the garage so you can wash the cars in winter or hose out leaves and dirt in the summer.

In case of fire: Most fire regulations require that the door between the garage and the house be fireproof, with a fire rating. Not that there is much danger of a car catching fire, but people generally store a lot of inflammable things in the garage.

Fire regulations also require that the garage floor be lower than the house floor by three steps or a specified distance established by the building code in your area.

Attic

The attic space will have to be thoroughly investigated before you can decide whether to make it into livable rooms. Whether you do or not depends on the head room, the floor construction, and the location of the stairs.

If the attic is low and made of prefabricated trusses, the chances of making it into habitable rooms are slim. Each member of a truss is a structural support and cannot be cut or eliminated. Prefabricated trusses have been used predominantly for development houses and are better not tampered with, unless you want to add an entire floor and reuse the trusses intact for the roof structure.

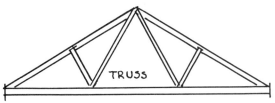

A prefabricated truss.

Head room: In old-fashioned attics that were stick-built, the head room is determined by the height of the collar beams in the upper third of the roof structure. These may sometimes be raised if they are too low to permit clear passage through the attic at a reasonable height, but only someone experienced should do this sort of work. Most codes require ceiling height in habitable rooms to be a minimum of 7 feet 6 inches; if the collar beams permit this height, you can consider using the space even if the finished ceiling is placed on top of the collar beams and they project down into the room.

Conventional attic space.

Flooring: Another determining factor is the construction of the attic floor and the size of the floor joists. The floor must be able to support the new load of furniture and people. Since an attic floor is usually not designed to carry very much additional weight, the joists may be only 2 by 6 inches. Depending on the span (the distance between the supporting structural walls below), these existing floor joists may not be heavy enough for the added weight. However, it may be possible to reinforce them with extra, and heavier, joists. If this is not done, the ceiling below could sag and the floor would, at best, be very bouncy. At worst, it could collapse.

Stairs: The third thing to examine is the stairway to the attic. Will there be adequate head room? Are the stairs in good condition, with safe handrails and easy risers? Do they land in the attic so the space can be developed without a lot of partitions? Are they in a good location as far as the first-floor circulation is concerned? For instance, they could be off the kitchen or back door. This might be all right if all you want to use the attic for is a child's playroom, but if you are going to make the attic into guest rooms or a master bedroom and bath, it will be a drawback if the approach to the attic cannot be made attractive and inviting. The stairs should be the deciding factor if the head room and the structure are adequate.

Perhaps new stairs can be built off the entrance hall to make remodeling the attic worthwhile. New stairs to the attic are not too difficult to build if the present stairs are steep and contain winders, as so many attic stairs do. If the stairs are hard to climb, you will use the attic space less no matter what you do with it, so building new and comfortable stairs should be considered. If you install a new circular stair from a more convenient location, leave the old stairs as a second exit, in case of fire.

The location of the bathroom downstairs will be a determining factor in the location of a bathroom in the attic. The new bath does not have to be directly over the old, but the wet wall should be continued through to the attic. Either side of the wet wall can be used

Dormers at left are shed roof and flush shed roof dormers.
Below (left to right) are the hipped (hip roof), gable (dog house), and flat (flat roof) dormers.

for the plumbing fixtures in the attic, depending on which gives you the best and most usable space.

If the chimney goes straight through the middle of the attic, it will have to be designed around, although not necessarily enclosed. The same is true of vent stacks from other plumbing fixtures. If they pass through the attic just where you want to have a dormer, you can enclose them and extend them through the dormer roof if they do not interfere with the function of the room. If they cannot be built around, they can be moved to a new location where they are out of the way.

Windows: Placed simply in the gable ends of the attic, windows may not provide enough light. If more light and air is needed, you can gain it, and additional space, with dormers.

Shed dormers can expand the usable floor space by at least 50 percent, and they are the least expensive dormer to build. Shed dormers are usually begun at the third rafter from each gable end. The new outside wall can either be built flush with the wall below for maximum floor space, or it can be set back a distance. The latter method will lose you some floor space, but it may look better from outside.

You may only want to use a shed dormer on the back of the house and, because of the scale of the facade, smaller doghouse or single-windowed shed dormers on the front. This method provides good cross ventilation. A small eyebrow dormer in a bathroom is better than no light or ventilation at all.

Use the same style window for the dormers as is used on the other floors of the house so the dormers do not look pieced-on or haphazard. Sliding glass doors can be used in the gable ends, or with a flush-shed dormer if a small balcony is designed with it for safety and so that the glass can be washed from the outside.

Glass or plastic skylights can be installed for light and ventilation if you do not need more floor space or additional head room. Glass skylights are more apt to leak. If not made from insulating glass, condensation will form on them and run down the ceiling, un-

A single shed roof dormer (top) *and an eyebrow dormer* (bottom).

Plastic skylights are delivered in a protective paper coating (top) *which should not be removed until skylight is installed and adjacent work completed.*

less a condensate drip is provided. Double plastic, or insulated plastic, skylights will not form condensation and they can be vented to furnish fresh air and circulation—which is difficult to get with glass. However, plastic skylights are far from perfect and have been known to crack. They scratch very easily; when delivered, they have a protective coating of heavy paper, which should not be removed until the skylight is completely installed in the roof and all the work to and around it has been completed. Over the years, wind, rain, dust, and the sun will fog them, and they tend to yellow with age. If you use skylights on the south slope of a roof, be sure the attic can be vented properly, because even in winter they can heat up the attic to an uncomfortable degree on a sunny day.

Insulation: Full insulation of the roof is required to conserve heat in winter and to keep the attic cooler in summer. The gable ends should be insulated, and insulating glass is desirable in any window located in the attic.

Heating the attic in winter is not as big a problem as air-conditioning it in summer since heat rises. With proper ventilation and insulation, you probably will not need more than a window unit or two in the summer, and a simple ventilating fan at the ridge may be enough.

Hot-water heat does not present the problems forced warm air does because the supply and return pipes are small and can be easily snaked through partitions. Warm-air ducts are much larger and will have to be taken from the furnace, through the lower floors, to the attic; the same is true of the return ducts. These can be boxed out on the lower floors, which is usually less expensive than cutting the plates and running the ducts through the partitions. Electric heat is simple and inexpensive to install, but very expensive to operate.

The walls and ceiling of the attic should be finished off the same as any other room in the house. If you want the extra height of a cathedral ceiling, simply put dry wall around the collar beams, leaving them exposed, and carry the dry wall to the ridge.

Basement

We tend to think of basements as damp, moldy places full of dark corners, grimy bottles, and boxes. Well, it is true that most basements fit that description. They are damp, low-ceilinged, sunless spaces nobody even wants to visit let alone live in. But a basement can be made into usable and attractive living space, though you must first consider who is going to be using it and how.

Seeping water or dampness: First, the basement must be dry. Most basements are not because drainage for rainwater from roofs and walls has not been provided for. Surrounding the perimeter of your house, at the level of the bottom of the footing, there should be a drain tile set in gravel to collect and carry water away from the house and foundation. The exterior of the basement walls should have been waterproofed with tar and felt when the drain tile was put in during the construction of the house. If these things were not done when the house was built, it will be expensive to have them done now.

It is possible, however, that the moisture in the basement is coming from inside the house, from a clothes dryer and washing machine, wet wash, leaking pipes, or condensation. Too, it may be coming from a hydrostatic head of water caused by a high water table in your area, and if so, there is very little you can do about it and it would be a mistake to remodel the basement unless you are prepared for a lot of extra expense.

A basement that is just normally damp may be waterproofed from the inside, depending on the cause and how bad it is. Do not be taken in by someone selling some new, almost magic, basement wall damp-proofer. It is not that easy or simple. In fact, very few reputable contractors will guarantee a waterproofing job on an existing basement. You can have all the foundation planting temporarily moved, the foundation excavated to the bottom of the footing, the tar and felt put on the wall, the drain tile run all around the exterior perimeter, the soil backfilled, and the foundation planting replaced. But you will have to decide yourself if it is worth it.

Remodeling of house above (left) consists of new double-hung windows to increase light and air circulation in basement area and a terrace which provides an attractive and useful outside living space.

Head room: The height of the basement is the second thing to consider. If you are going to make a room down there, you will want a finished ceiling to cover the ducts and plumbing. Low ceilings are especially depressing in a basement because they seem to make you feel that the weight of the house is pressing down on you. There may be one or two sections where the ceiling must be as low as 6 feet 8 inches, which is all right since that is the height of most doors, but the entire ceiling should not be that low.

Because of the ducts, pipes, and the barely adequate head room, most basements are difficult to remodel. One possibility is to lower the floor level. This is not complicated or hard to do, but it takes doing. Temporary supports must be put in to shore up the joists of the floor above. The furnace and other equipment may be left where they are, but in other areas the concrete floor will have to be broken up and taken out. A new footing and foundation wall is then built in from the existing basement wall. The earth is excavated to the desired level and taken out. New footings are dug and poured for the new Lally columns that are to be the permanent support for the floor joists, and a new concrete floor is poured. The

whole operation can take as little as three weeks or as long as three months.

Stairs: The third thing to consider is the location of the stairs. Ideally, they should be in or just off the front entrance hall. Too often they are by the back door in the kitchen, which is a poor location if you want to have a recreation room in the basement since you may have to herd guests past the sink.

If the basement stairs are not in a good location, do not attempt an expensive remodeling of the basement without providing a good entrance to it.

The stairs should be open and inviting, with easy risers. They should be wide, well lighted, and you should not have to wind through the living room, dining room, and kitchen to get to them. If they must at times be closed off from the main floor, use wide double doors that have glass or louvers in them to avoid a "back stairs" atmosphere.

Whether the basement is to be used only for storage or also for other purposes, there should be two exits: one up the stairs and through the house, and the other directly to the outside. This is an advantage when moving furniture and equipment in and out, and mandatory as a safety measure in case of fire.

Former crawl space is made into a full-height basement (left) *by excavating and removing earth through opening under living room window. Finished remodeling* (right) *is invisible.*

This basement light well, topped with a plastic skylight, allows enough light and ventilation for growing plants to flourish in an otherwise unlikely location.

Windows: The fourth, and almost the most important, thing to consider is the sunlight and ventilation the basement gets or that you can arrange for it to have. There is no point in spending money to create a room of any sort if the only natural light and ventilation is through the typical dinky basement windows. Even if the room is to be used mostly at night (and what room can you afford to use only after dark?), it should have generous windows. All the photographs of finished basements in magazines and advertisements have the same fault, regardless of how expensive the furniture or what the quality of the carpeting —they have typical basement windows and are still basements.

You do not need all that earth piled up around the basement walls. Dig it out and increase the size of the windows. There are several ways you can do this.

You can enlarge the window by using a light well, which is an area dug out around the window with a drain in it to prevent the buildup of water. It should be painted white to reflect as much light as possible into the basement, and can be made of masonry, metal, or plastic. Usually the metal and plastic is corrugated for added strength in keeping the earth away from the light well. If snow is a problem, you can cover the well with a see-through plastic dome made for this purpose.

If you want, you can insulate the light well, make it 6 feet deep, and cover it with an insulated dome, thus doing away with the window altogether. Even if it gets no sunlight at

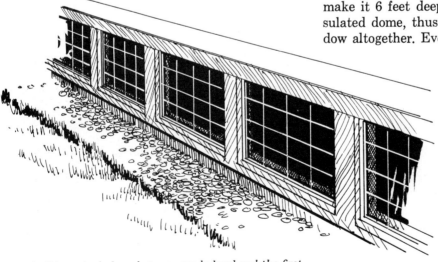

A ribbon of windows between grade level and the first floor provides light to basement area.

all, there are still many plants you can grow at the base of it all year round.

You can remove the basement wall for a good distance on the south side, supporting the floor joist with columns, and make a whole section of ribbon windows to admit sunlight into the basement. If the south side is also the front of the house, you can still do this if you build a ramped bridge to the front door. For privacy, ventilation, and maximum sunlight, relocate the foundation planting away from the windows or at the front lot line.

You can, if you choose, go all the way and remove the earth to a point below the basement floor, creating a sunken terrace and garden off the basement that can be reached through sliding glass doors in the basement and an exterior stair made of concrete blocks from the upper level. The footing of the basement may have to be deepened to below the frost line, and the terrace should slope to a drain. A low fence or wall should be enough protection at grade level until hedges and shrubbery grow large enough to keep toddlers away. If you are at all security conscious, this is also an excellent way of keeping strangers away from large open-glass areas, if the stairs from grade level are omitted.

Sliding glass doors on the main floor can be protected with a narrow balcony, which will be useful when washing the glass on the outside. If your house is on a hillside, the solution is much simpler and you may only have to build one retaining wall instead of three.

If no underground obstructions exist, a well-drained sunken terrace off the basement can open it to light and air.

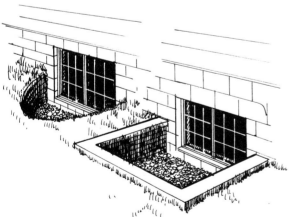

Individual basement windows can be enlarged by using light wells.

When basement lighting is crucial, a bridge can be built to provide access to the house.

Use of area: After you have decided that you can and want to remodel your basement, consider who is going to use it and for what purpose.

A workshop? Even a mildly damp basement can be used for a shop of sorts, but all the material and supplies have to be hauled down there (not too much of a problem with an exterior exit). Remember, the noise from power saws and other electrical equipment will carry all through the house, and paint, wood, and other materials could create a fire hazard.

A recreation room? Who is going to play there, children or adults? Children will not mind tramping through the kitchen to get there, but perhaps you will. And adult guests may get the feeling that you are taking them to the basement for cocktails or bridge so they will not mess up the carpeting and good furniture in your living room.

A study or a den in the basement may provide a quiet, out-of-the-way place to work and read, if it is not located under the kitchen or a noisy room. But the basement must be dry because dampness is very harmful to books.

A bedroom or two in the basement is also a possibility—again, only if it is dry. You must have a clear height of at least 7 feet 6 inches, low windows for plenty of sunlight and ventilation, a good staircase from the floor above, and a safe exit to the outdoors from the basement. A basement will not do as a bedroom for elderly people. They will complain about the dampness even if it is as dry as a bone. They will also complain about the cold, the stairs, and the noise overhead. Psychologically, it is all wrong for them; being underground is something they want to avoid thinking about.

So before you go all out on basement remodeling, think hard about how you will use it. Unless you can come up with a really good design for a room that will be used by the whole family for the purpose intended, it might be better to invest the money in another part of the house.

Every basement should contain a second, emergency exit, even if it means the use of unattractive and inconvenient hatch doors.

8
Buildings into Homes

Up to this point we have been speaking mostly about remodeling houses to make them better homes. However, there are other possibilities, other structures, that can be made into homes and apartments. An old garage at the back of your property, for instance, could be converted into a house or apartment without too much trouble if it is in good condition and the zoning ordinances permit it. (Some zoning ordinances will not permit two kitchens on the same lot.) The structure and the floor are there; what is needed is insulation, plumbing, electricity, heat, and finishing. Many old detached garages go unused because they are away from the house, or because the doors, the size of the garage, and the location make them inconvenient for today's automobiles. A one-car garage will limit you to a studio apartment or guest room, though it would also make an excellent retreat for a retired executive who is used to working in an office. Many retired men find that being in the house all day is more irritating and strenuous than they thought it would be. They need a private place to escape to, even if it is only on Thursday afternoons when their wives' bridge club arrives.

Many buildings can be moved if you cannot buy the land and remodel them where they stand. The cost of moving a structure depends not so much on the size as on the number of telephone and light wires that must be cut to move it through the streets to a new site. Old barns, garages, gasoline stations, and any number of other buildings can be bought cheaply, on the condition that the buyer remove them from the site within so many days.

Gas Stations

A gasoline station could make an excellent home if it is in a residential section, as so many of them used to be. With the oil shortage, many are being closed and put up for sale (the property may have been leased or bought outright). They can be moved or made into homes right where they stand. Heat, electricity, and plumbing have already been installed, and the unusually large spaces for servicing automobiles can be turned into handsome living areas. Some that had hydraulic lifts are high enough to be divided into two floors, or a balcony and sleeping loft. You will probably want to remove much of the paving except what you need for your own garage, and the gasoline storage tanks should be removed before you remodel.

Schoolhouses

With the consolidation of education so prevalent, small schoolhouses are being abandoned. These can easily be turned into homes.

A gasoline or service station (top) can be remodeled into an attractive and unusual residence (bottom). Two of the service bays are retained as a garage, and a service porch and protected side entrance are added on the right.

They may be auctioned off or sold directly by sealed bids. Some are hardly little red schoolhouses; they are large brick two-story buildings that can be turned into apartment houses with a little imagination. The zoning laws will determine whether you can do this (schools used to be built in residential neighborhoods). One thing that should be investigated in either a large or a small schoolhouse is the heating system. Most old schools had a custodian who spent a lot of his time in the furnace room, and unless you want to do that too, you will probably have to replace the heating system with a modern residential one. The electric wiring will have to be changed, too, because schools will not have the convenience outlets a residence requires.

Churches

A church can sometimes be bought and made into a very exciting home. Most are in residential areas, and some have had years of congregational care lavished on them. Again, the plumbing, heating, and electrical work will have to be redone before a house of worship can be used as a house to live in. Some churches will already have kitchens, but usually these are in the basement near the meeting and social rooms. If there is a balcony in the church, there will already be a staircase and all or part of the nave can be made into second-floor bedrooms—not that this should be done in every case. Many times you can take advantage of the long narrow windows and turn the high-ceilinged nave into a very impressive living room.

Barns

An old barn is everyone's dream to remodel into a house. Usually a barn is situated in the quiet countryside, where you want to live, and the massive timbers, weathered siding, and romantic roots to the past make them very desirable homes. Barns are really not that easy to remodel, however, because sometimes the spaces are too big to handle easily. The structure should have been well taken care of—the roof repaired, the masonry caulked, and the hayloft cleaned. Too often there are rotting beams, sinking foundations, termites and other vermin, and homeless field mice who found the place before you did.

A barn will require everything needed to build a house, with the exception of those beautiful old beams and barn siding, which almost do not exist anymore. It will take longer to remodel than a conventional house because barn structures age differently. It will have settled and sagged, and there will be few straight lines or square corners. The siding will probably have to be battened to close the cracks; the roof will need to be replaced; and you will need insulation, windows, doors, plumbing, heating, electricity, water, septic tanks, and finishing materials for floors, walls, and ceilings. None of this stops anyone who has his eye on a barn from buying it and making it into an exciting and fascinating place to live.

Other buildings, such as mills, railroad stations, small factories, blacksmith shops, and foundries, can be remodeled into homes, Some vision is needed, but do not think that just because it was not built as a house, it cannot be made into a home.

Everyone dreams of transforming an old barn (top) *into a home. Here, the old barn doors have been left to enclose an entrance courtyard and can be closed in bad weather. For additional protection, the light well could be glassed over.*

9
Planning Your Utilities

With the exception of electricity—which has only been harnessed within the last hundred years—indoor plumbing, central heating, and one form of air conditioning or another have been making houses more comfortable since the days of ancient Rome. Electricity has made it easier to light homes at night, just as it has made the mechanical operation of furnaces, air conditioners, and the pumps on which plumbing depends more efficient. But what we have failed to do, and what has made us so dependent on electricity today, is to use the natural energy of the sun for light and heat, and the prevailing breeze, and trees and vines for cooling. Before remodeling, the mechanical systems of the house should be brought up to their maximum capacity and be working as efficiently as possible. Then the remodeling should incorporate the time-honored, natural energy-saving design ideas that existed before the birth of Christ to make our homes brighter by day, warmer in winter, and cooler in summer.

Heating

There are three basic ways to heat a home: forced warm air, using registers; hot water, using radiators; and radiant heat, using hot-water pipes cast in concrete. All have their advantages and disadvantages.

Registers: Forced warm air heats a house quickly, and can be humidified in winter for a healthier atmosphere. In this system, a fan at the furnace forces warm air through ducts into the rooms, and a return duct takes the air back to the furnace where it is filtered to remove dust and cooking odors. Forced warm air can be a fuel waster because all the air in the room must be warmed before the occupants are comfortable, and large areas of glass can cause cold down drafts. Properly installed, it is relatively silent, although it is not a good idea to locate the furnace under bedrooms, where the noise when it is activated by thermostat at night, could be disturbing.

Most furnaces can handle the addition of a room or two if you add or extend the ducts and rebalance the system. Even if the present furnace is working to capacity, you may be able to heat a modest addition by insulating the new and existing ducts, weatherstripping all the doors and windows, and using insulating glass and heavier than normal insulation.

Perimeter heating, the practice of placing registers under doors and windows along the outside walls, is good practice if they are far enough from the wall not to be obscured by curtains or drapery. Do not place ducts behind or under furniture. A return duct in every room except the bathroom is ideal, but expensive.

Radiators: Hot-water heating, or hydronic heating, does not compare in many ways with forced warm air. It can make the atmosphere of the house very hot and dry in winter, and this system cannot circulate or filter the air. If air conditioning is desired, separate ducts and equipment must be added. Hot-water heat does lend itself to remodeling since the pipes are small and can easily be run through existing walls. Household hot water can, and should, be incorporated into the system for unlimited supplies of hot water.

The one-pipe system is the least effective because hot water running through the pipe heats the first radiator the hottest, and cools down as it runs along to other radiators. A two-pipe system, which returns the water from each radiator separately so that each receives heat at approximately the same temperature, provides uniform heat.

Radiator covers should be designed so that cool air can circulate around the radiator through a space next to the floor at the bottom of the cover, and out again through a grill over the front of the radiator. Covers should be removable in case the radiator needs servicing.

New radiators are more efficient than the old-fashioned stand-up kind. Cast iron is the best material for radiators because it retains the heat longer and distributes it better. Aluminum radiators are noisy because of their rapid rate of expansion and do not retain heat well. Baseboard radiators running along the floor on exterior walls permit you to place furniture against all walls, but some models are bulky and unsightly.

Radiant heat: With this system, hot water is circulated in pipes imbedded in the concrete floor, warming the entire mass of floor and radiating heat to the occupants of the room without warming the air. Radiant heat uses the same principle as solar heat—the rays of the sun pierce millions of miles of cold space to warm the earth. If you already have hot-water heat, you can install radiant heat in a new addition. It is expensive to install, but economical to operate. It is also slow to warm up and slow to cool down, a disadvantage in rapidly changing climates.

Problem-solving tips: Many things can go wrong with any system. Whichever one you choose should be installed and working properly before or during the remodeling. If dust and soot come out of your warm-air registers or if you smell oil, call your furnace man at once. You should not be able to smell oil or see smoke coming from the chimney. Either indicates that the furnace is not working at full capacity and is wasting fuel.

Most radiators make some noise, but anything unusual should be investigated. If half the radiator is hot while the other half is cold, something is blocking the flow of hot water. It could be that air is trapped in the radiator and needs to be released. Metallic paint reduces the efficiency of a radiator. It should be repainted with an oil-base paint.

New furnaces are more efficient and compact than the older ones, but those with fans, pumps, and blowers can be noisy. Discuss the placement of a new furnace with a heating contractor. A central location will require fewer ducts or pipes and will heat the rooms faster with less fuel and heat loss. New prefabricated chimneys have Fire Underwriters approval, so you are no longer tied to the masonry chimney.

If you are putting the new furnace in the basement, you can save space by placing the oil tank in the ground outside the house. Small tanks of 225 gallons have to be filled often in the winter months. If you are getting a new tank, get one holding a minimum of 550 gallons. A 1,000-gallon tank is even better because you can have it filled in the summer when rates may be lower.

If noise from your furnace is a problem, you can insulate the basement ceiling or build a furnace room—but do not wall up the furnace in a tight enclosure because it needs fresh air containing oxygen to burn fuel efficiently. You should leave enough space around it so that it can be easily serviced.

The electrical contractor should install safety switches so the furnace can be turned off quickly in an emergency. Radiators should be capable of being drained and turned off individually so that when you want to conserve fuel by closing off several unused rooms, you can do it easily.

Antifreeze instead of water in a hot-water system will prevent pipes and radiators from freezing if the electricity goes off when you are not at home. With antifreeze, you will not have to drain the system if you go away for the winter.

Thermostats: Place the thermostat on an inside wall, away from the warm kitchen, direct sunlight, and cold drafts. Though the contractor usually wants to put the thermostat right over the sofa in the living room, this is seldom the best location, particularly if the front door is in the living room. If you do not want the thermostat where the contractor wants to put it, the utility company in your area will help you decide the best location. For better control, you can set up separately zoned areas (each with its own thermostat) to be heated only when needed.

Thermostats may be equipped with a clock timer that will turn the heat on automatically a half-hour before your usual rising time in the morning. You can comfortably save fuel this way, because the house will be cool at night while you are sleeping, and warm in the morning when you wake up.

Fuel: Electricity, oil, and gas are the three most common forms of fuel. The best one for your house depends on the area in which you live. In a house with an existing heating system that does not need replacement, it is probably best to go along with what you already have.

Electric heating is the cheapest to install because you do not need a tank, chimney, vent, or ductwork, but it is the most expensive to operate. Since there is only one utility company in your area, you have no bargaining power over the rates and must pay up or freeze. However, if everything in your house runs on electricity, the companies will usually give you a special discount rate.

Heating by oil does give you the advantage of being able to shop around for fuel, and if you have a large storage tank (say, enough for the whole winter's supply), you will not be subject to fluctuating prices. However, if supplies run low, the fuel companies will furnish oil to regular customers first.

Gas heating rates may be competitive with those for oil, if both fuels are available in your area, and costs less to install because you need no storage tank. Gas is metered into your house just as electricity is. You are similarly at the mercy of the gas company as far as rates are concerned, because you cannot stock up as you can with oil. And regardless of all the safeguards, gas is the most dangerous fuel.

Liquid petroleum (usually shortened to LP gas) can be used for heating, and since there are usually several companies that supply the LP tanks, rates can be competitive. But again, if there is a shortage, the companies supply their regular customers first.

Air Conditioning

Used to air-conditioned offices, cars, trains, buses, theaters, restaurants, and stores, many people feel they cannot get through the summer without air conditioning in their homes. But if your house is properly designed to begin with—with cross ventilation, overhangs, vents and interior fans, heavy insulation on the inside, the right foundation plantings, trees that shade windows, and heat-reflecting colors on the outside—you will find that you can get by with no, or minimum, air conditioning.

Central air conditioning helps keep your house cleaner, quieter, and free of pollen and dust, especially if you live on a busy street in a crowded neighborhood with no big trees around. But if you live in the middle of suburban lawns and trees, it is a mistake to install all that equipment unless it is absolutely necessary.

It is also sad that as we grow more security conscious, the traditional ways of summer living are changing. Many people are afraid to sleep in first-floor bedrooms with open doors and windows protected only by a flimsy screen. Locked doors and windows the year round are not luxuries, but necessities for their comfort, safety and peace of mind. Thus air conditioning becomes essential.

Before you consider air conditioning too seriously, consult with your local utility company to see if your present electric service can take on the added load. A 200-ampere service is usually needed for central air conditioning, but some 100-ampere systems can supply the power for several individual room units.

Central: Central air conditioning is divided into three basic types: single package, split system, and a combination of heating and air conditioning.

Single-package systems combine fans, compressor, condenser, and evaporator in a single unit, which goes inside the house. It is not a large unit and can be fitted into attics, crawl spaces, or a closet if necessary. It is noisy, and should be installed on pads to reduce the vibration throughout the house.

With the split system of air conditioning, the noisiest part of the system, the condenser, is placed on a concrete foundation outside the house. It should not be near a bedroom window because it will make enough noise to be heard through the windowpane.

Combined heating and air conditioning is the best system if you are installing a new forced warm air furnace and ducts. You may either include air conditioning now, or add it later.

Any central air conditioning work requires an air conditioning engineer, top-quality insulation, and adequate electrical service.

One room: Individual room air conditioners may be acceptable when you want only one or two rooms to be cooled. Place them in the walls where they will be quieter, air- and watertight, and permanent. Window air conditioners allow a lot of cooled air to escape, make more noise, block your view, are not watertight, and prevent the window from being locked.

Remember, though, even these small units require that you go over your electrical service first to see if it can carry the extra load. Most units need special wiring, and all should be grounded.

Wiring and Lighting

Inadequate wiring and electrical service is something that all older (and some newer) homes have in common, unless they have been rewired by previous owners. We may not know exactly what electricity *is*, but we do know what it does and how it works.

Water runs through a pipe and is measured by the gallon; electricity flows through wires and is measured by the ampere. Water pressure is measured in gallons per minute; the pressure of electricity is measured by the volts or voltage, and the voltage times the amperes is the unit of electric power called watts.

Electricity needs: If you have a 100-ampere, 240-volt system coming into your house, you have a capacity of 24,000 watts—the very minimum required for a small house today. That may sound like a lot of electricity, but it is not when you consider that the average electric range uses from 8,000 to 16,000 watts.

Many codes require you to upgrade all the electricity in your home if a new area is added or if you do any remodeling that involves electrical wiring. This includes the installation of electric convenience outlets every 12 feet around the walls in every room in both the old and the new sections of the house. If you plan to add air conditioning or electric heating, or a number of electrical appliances, it costs very little more to put in a 200-ampere, 240-volt service, which would provide you with a capacity of 48,000 watts. This is called a "three-wire service."

In a three-wire service there are two wires, each carrying 120 volts, and a third wire that grounds the service as a safety measure. These go to a fuse box or, more recently, to a circuit breaker. The old fuse boxes were often inconvenient and dangerous—inconvenient if you did not have the correct fuse to replace the burnt-out one, and dangerous if you used one too large for the wiring, allowing too much electricity to pass into the wires (the cause of many electrical fires).

Many new codes require a circuit breaker, which will trip off when the circuit is overloaded. When the offending fixture is found and the circuit is safe to use, you can simply push the circuit switch to "on" and everything functions again.

For general illumination, each area of your house will have its own circuit of 1,000 watts, with not more than ten outlets for lighting fixtures. Wattages are stamped on light bulbs and all small appliances, so it is easy for you to add them up so you do not overload the circuit. Each room should be on two different circuits so that if one goes out, the room will not be in total darkness.

Appliance circuits: All major appliances should have their own separate circuit of 120 and 240 volts and each should be grounded.

120 volts	240 volts
refrigerator	electric range
refrigerator freezer	built-in cook top
washing machine	oven
dishwasher	dryer
garbage disposal	electric water heater
freezer	water pump
furnace	
water pump	

All electrical work should conform to local codes and to the National Electric Code prepared by the National Board of Fire Underwriters. If all the electrical wiring does not conform to the code and there is a fire due to faulty wiring, you may not be able to collect the fire insurance.

Switches and outlets: Three-way switches are a great convenience and will prevent many accidents if placed at the top and bottom of each stairway and at opposite ends of halls.

Each room should have a light switch at the door which controls at least one light in the room. In the kitchen, it is usually the light over the sink; in the dining room, it is the light over the table; in the living room, it is the lights on each side of the sofa; in the bedroom, it is the light on the dressing table or

bureau. In a bedroom, never control a ceiling light or bedside lamps from the door switch. If you are sharing the room with someone and they are asleep, you risk tripping over something in the dark if you do *not* turn on the light, and the anger of the awakened sleeper if you *do*.

Convenience outlets should be planned around furniture placement or you will find they are in unreachable places behind sofas and beds. Their placement is governed by code, but only as a minimum standard and with some latitude.

Plumbing

Plumbing in older homes seems to live a life of its own, separate from the house and the family who share the house with it. It can rattle, breathe, knock, shake, work, or go on vacation at the worst possible time. But just because it is old, you do not have to put it out to pasture. The replacement may or may not be better.

Your plumbing begins either at the connection to the city main or your own well, and it is easier to get into the house than to get out. If you are connecting to a city main, you may be limited to ¾-inch connections. For a small one-bathroom house, that may be sufficient. But if you plan to have two or more baths, a dishwasher, and other water-using equipment, additional taps will be needed. The number will be governed by the code in your area so there is no guessing about it.

Wells: A private well used to be a good source of pure, clean, and abundant water, but with crowded neighborhoods, detergents, and sewage pollution, fresh drinking water is difficult to find. Hire only the most reputable well driller, because even he can only assure you of water—not the quality of the water. In most towns and suburbs, where you can drill for water is controlled by code to ensure you a safe supply. In other words, you must be a certain distance from your own and from your neighbors' cesspools and septic tanks.

A well costs so much per foot in depth; some communities mandate a minimum depth, whether you strike good water before that depth or not. Begin with a good well driller and get a written contract, unit prices, and a report of the depth, size of well casing, size of filter screen, and yield per hour. You will need 6 to 8 gallons per minute for the average home. The water is tested after continuous pumping for at least twenty-four hours.

Insulate the water storage tank, especially if it is in the basement, to prevent condensation. A small tank with a small pump will operate more frequently and wear out more quickly on a 2-inch well than on a 4-inch well with a submersible pump. The submersible pump, since it is in the bottom of the well, is noiseless. A water pump in the basement from a 2-inch well can be very distracting because it will go on and off all the time.

The submersible pump and 4-inch well will cost twice as much as a 2-inch well, but will last more than twice as long. They will not, however, assure you of better or purer water, which is more a matter of luck than knowledge.

Hard water: Water with a lot of minerals and rust in it, commonly called hard water, requires a filter and a water softener. Without them, the rust will stain the plumbing fixtures, your white laundry will come out brown, and the pipes will begin to clog up and eventually will have to be replaced.

Heating: A water heater adequate for your family should hold at least 30 to 40 gallons, and it should be glass lined and have a quick recovery so you will not run out of hot water. Check the gallons-per-person recommended by your utility company.

Plumbing traps: A trap between the house and sewer or septic tank, and one at each fixture, prevent sewage fumes from backing up and getting inside the house. Traps must be vented through vertical walls to the roof in what is called a wet wall, which contains these vents plus soil pipes, hot and cold supply lines, and drains. Architects prefer to cluster kitchen and bathroom fixtures around these wet walls to save money on the plumbing. Before you tie into the existing drain or waste stack, be sure that it is properly vented and is of adequate size to handle the increased load.

Faucets: Cold-water faucets are always on the right side of a sink and turn clockwise to open. Hot-water faucets are always on the left and turn counterclockwise to open. Never try to change this arrangement. Although it is only a convention established through custom, any other composition will be confusing and may cause hand-washing guests to scald themselves.

A leaking faucet is not as disturbing as other plumbing noises, unless you are trying to sleep. Faucet leaks are usually caused by worn washers, which are not difficult to replace providing you have the correct washer. Nothing is standard in plumbing, but you can arm yourself with a boxed assortment of washers at any hardware store—one of them will probably fit. Just be sure to turn off the valve under the sink before you remove the cap and spindle of the faucet or you will have water all over. If a new washer does not fix the leak, the faucet needs a new seat, which should be put in by a plumber.

When a faucet vibrates, it means the water pressure is reacting against loose parts, usually the seat. A high-pitched whistle is caused by a worn valve or washer that is not allowing the faucet to close properly.

Plumbing noise: Water hammer results when pipes in floors shudder as the faucet is turned off and is usually due to one of two things: either the pipe is not the correct size (this can be corrected by a shock absorber), or the water is traveling some distance through sagging lines and moves back and forth when the flow is turned off. This can break the joints, but it is easily corrected by leveling sagging lines with hangers padded with plastic foam and by installing a shock absorber.

Hot-water lines knock when the temperature in the water heater gets above 140° F., creating steam that is trapped there. This can be dangerous. You should check the temperature and keep it under 140° F.

When a water pump goes on every time a toilet is flushed, the air pressure in the storage tank is too high to allow enough water to remain in the tank. Eventually this will cause the pump to burn out a bearing.

10
Conserving Fuel and Energy

As you plan your remodeling, there are many features you can incorporate into the design to save fuel and electricity and keep a warmer house in winter and a cooler one in summer. Very few of these fuel-saving suggestions involve structural changes, and those that do are minor.

Insulation

Insulation is one of the first devices used to maintain a stable temperature within the house year round. In winter, it retains, and can reflect, heat in the house, and in summer, it can keep heat out, if you and your house work along with it. The three most common forms of insulation, and the easiest to install in an existing house, are batts, granular insulation, and rigid styrofoam. You should never use any form of insulation that is not fire*proof* (fire-*resistant* is not sufficient), waterproof, and vermin- and rot-proof.

Insulating batts: Also called blankets, batts are made of mineral wool, fiberglass, perlite, or vermiculite, with a vapor barrier on one side (it should face the interior of the house). Aluminum foil may be used on one side of the batt to reflect heat back into the room, or if you live in a warm climate, on the side of the batt away from the room to reflect heat to the exterior and cut the cost of air conditioning. The batts come in various thicknesses and in widths of 12 to 24 inches. They are purchased in large bundles, which are unrolled between studs and joists. This is not difficult or expensive on new construction, or where you can get to the studs or joists, but insulating an existing wall that is finished is not quite so easy or inexpensive.

Older homes may be insulated from the interior or the exterior. If the interior walls are in poor condition and must be redone, then it is best to remove them and put the insulation between the studs and refinish the walls with Sheetrock. If the wall is plaster and you want to avoid the dust and dirt involved in removing it, furr out the walls over the old plaster, insulate, and refinish the walls. Remember, however, that the room will be decreased in size by the thickness of the new walls. Doors and windows will have to be boxed-out and possibly retrimmed. It is expensive to move radiators out from the wall, so they will have to be boxed around too. You can save heat from the radiator by placing reflective insulation (just thin aluminum foil) behind the radiators.

You can insulate from the exterior, but this method is very expensive because it requires new siding, painting, resetting, and flashing of doors and windows if the exterior wall is furred out for batts. If you need new siding, then insulation can be incorporated with it.

Materials: Insulated aluminum siding (see Chapter 11) does not require the doors and windows to be reset and flashed due to the thinness of the siding and insulation. Check the R-value rating of the insulation before you make a choice.

Granular insulation can be either perlite or vermiculite. It comes in large bags and is most effectively used to insulate unfloored attics, where it is simply spread between the joists. It can also be used to insulate existing exterior walls; it is then blown through a hole made in the siding between each stud. Because of wiring, plumbing, heating ducts, and other unseen obstructions, this expensive process is rarely worth the effort, and is only as good as the man who installs it.

Styrofoam insulation, in sheet form, comes in different widths and thicknesses. It can be very effective to insulate old interior walls. It needs no furring and can be nailed or glued to the wall. The wall must then be refinished with new plasterboard or paneling. Styrofoam is expensive and its main attraction is that it is easy to work with and the thin sheets do not cut into the room size as other insulation does.

R-value: The effectiveness of insulation is not related to its thickness, but to its resistance to heat flow. The higher the R-value rating of an insulation, the more effective it is. The R-value should be stamped on all insulation you buy. The minimum R-value for walls is 11; for ceilings, 19; and for floors over crawl spaces, 13.

Insulation should be used between any heated and unheated space within the house, especially in floors or rooms over garages or porches.

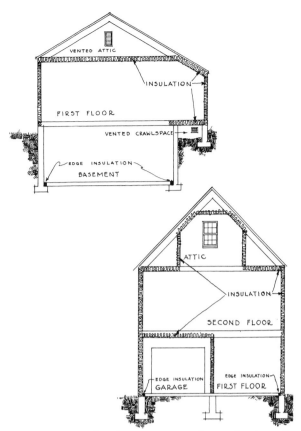

Insulation location in a one-story house (top) *and in a two-and-a-half-story house with interior garage* (bottom).

Windows

Much more air leakage occurs around windows than through them. The solution is weatherstripping and caulking around the exterior trim. The same solution applies to doors, although large sliding glass doors or windows can cause down drafts and draw heat from the room to their cold surfaces. Condensation, forming on the glass, can run down the panes and damage the window and the sills. However, many of these problems can be avoided if you have an insulated lining on your drapes and keep them closed after dark —a good way to conserve heat in any room during the winter months.

Insulated glass: Composed of two sheets of glass with a sealed air space between, insulated glass will eliminate down drafts, fogging, and condensation. It costs one-third to one-half more than regular glass, but less than storm windows.

Storm windows: If good storm windows are properly installed, they cut heat loss. But if the window is not in good shape in the first place, storm windows will be more bother than they are worth. Then it is better to get new insulated glass windows. Storm windows can fog up, allow condensation to damage the sill, and, unless expertly installed, rattle all winter. Then there is the added nuisance of putting them up every fall and taking them down every spring. They also present double window-washing chores.

Insulating tips: If your house has some insulation but the walls still remain cold, you may be able to solve the problem in the living room or a bedroom by building a bookcase around the window and filling the wall with books. Dead air space is an excellent insulator. In a bathroom with a cold wall, build shallow cabinets just large enough to hold towels and bathroom accessories over the entire wall.

Kitchen cabinets will help insulate a cold kitchen wall. If plumbing pipes run through them, leave the cabinet doors open on freezing nights to allow warm air from the house to circulate around the pipes.

Designing for Conservation

Once a house has been constructed, it is difficult to change the location of rooms unless you do extensive remodeling, but if you are adding a room and want to conserve on fuel, the location of the room can make a difference.

Bathrooms, bedrooms, and kitchens on the east side of the house will warm up earlier, from the sun's rays, than rooms on the west side of the house, and you will save on electric bills by not having to turn on the lights most mornings. Too, sun coming into a bedroom and bath make them more pleasant areas to wake up and wash in, and a sunny kitchen is a happy place to have breakfast. Limit the size of windows on the north side of the house. If you live in the South and rely on air conditioning, use large glass windows on the north side.

If the new family room you are planning is going to be used more than the living room during the day, try to place it where it gets the most sunshine. The south side of the house is a good place for the room that gets the most use because in the winter it will heat up during the day, and you can retain the heat at night by drawing the drapes. Overhangs will keep out the summer sun.

It is always a good idea to have one window, even if it is small, on the western side of the kitchen and living room so you can catch the last rays of sunset. They do not carry much warmth in them, so they will not help to heat the house, but they will cast a lovely warm glow over the rooms.

If you are adding a room for an elderly relative, try to build it on the south side with exposures to the east and west. Sunshine makes people feel better.

There is little excuse for building any house, either in the North or the South, without front and rear entrance halls. In the North, they keep drafts and cold out of other rooms, and in the South, they help keep the heat out and the air-conditioned air in. Incorporate entrance halls in the front and back of the house in any remodeling you do.

Old, unused porches keep sunlight away from windows and the warmth of the sun out of the house. Foundation planting that has grown higher than the roof will also shield the windows from the sun in winter. In summer, overgrown foundation planting causes dampness and prevents air from circulating freely through the rooms. It should be removed or severely cut back.

High ceilings and tall windows help keep a room cool in the summer, if they are protected by overhangs to keep out the sun.

Franklin stoves, with exposed metal chimney flues, will heat a room in a matter of minutes much more efficiently than a conventional fireplace. They use very little fuel compared to the heat they produce, and you can warm things on the top and broil a whole dinner in the grate.

Venting skylights and clerestory windows facing south can heat a room with winter sunshine and cool it in summer by ventilating out warm air. They must be shaded by trees in the summer, though, or they will allow the room to become too hot.

11
Interior Renovating

When you are remodeling the interior of your house, do not take literally the glowing photographs and manufacturers' claims about some fantastic new product for floors, walls, or ceilings that is supposed to revolutionize housekeeping chores, make your day lighter, and your life brighter. Few products are really new, and those that are probably have defects that will show up later. Sliced bread is great, but it gets stale quickly. And yes, vinyl upholstery never needs cleaning, but when sewed on a cushion, the holes made by the needle make it as easy to tear as a sheet of perforated government stamps. Ignore all claims and seals of approval. Get a small amount of whatever it is you are thinking of using and test it yourself for durability, cleaning, scratching, bending, tearing, denting, and burning.

Walls

Partitions: Walls that divide space into rooms but do not support any weight of the structure are called partitions. They do brace and contribute to the general stability of the house in high winds or under unusual conditions, but they can be moved without endangering the house. They usually contain wiring, and may have plumbing and heating ducts in them, which must be considered if the partition is to be moved. Wiring can be disconnected, rerouted, or consolidated with plumbing and ductwork in one or more boxed columns. If the columns interfere with furniture placement or circulation in the newly opened space, the mechanical elements may be moved to the side and concealed in a pilaster. Hollow beams, columns, and pilasters should be oversized if they contain soil pipes so they can be insulated to deaden the sound of rushing water. Hardwood floors, tile, and Sheetrock or plaster stop at the wall, so be prepared for patching and refinishing when you remove a partition.

Structural: Load-bearing structural walls support the roof or additional floors, but may be moved or partially removed if suitable temporary and substitute permanent support can be found to replace them. They will also have wiring and perhaps plumbing and heating ducts in them. All the exterior walls of the house are structural, and there is usually one or more interior structural wall since joists seldom exceed 16 to 20 feet in length.

A series of columns supporting short spans of wood beams can be used, but if you want to remove a sizable length of structural wall, a steel beam should be substituted for the wall. Suitable support must be provided for the beam at each end of the span and foundation walls may have to be reinforced.

Large windows and sliding glass doors may be placed in exterior walls, but the walls and floors above must be supported in the same manner as when you remove a wall entirely.

Furring: Furring out a masonry wall in the basement or garage is relatively simple. Furring strips are attached to the masonry with special masonry nails. The strips themselves may be 1 by 2 inches, or they may be studs and pieces of studs left over from work on another part of the house. Plumb the wall to make certain it is straight, and be sure to have all the faces of the furring strips on the same plane, even if you have to cut the back of them to fit over irregularities in the masonry. Nail the finish wall to the furring strips. Some wallboard and prefinished plywood will not hold up well in a damp basement. When finishing off a basement make sure the materials you use are not sensitive to dampness.

New partitions are easy to erect using 2-by-4 studs with a sole plate of the same size at the bottom and one at top. The studs are cut to fit firmly between sole and top plate and are spaced 16 inches on center. If a soil pipe is to be run through the partition for a bathroom you are adding, 2-by-6 studs should be used.

Many materials are available for finishing the partition, but gypsum board or dry wall is the most popular and the least expensive. It is easy to work with and cut, and it is fireproof, but it must be taped and spackled before painting. Even if you want to finish the wall in prefinished plywood, it is better to apply dry wall first (in this case you do not have to tape and spackle it) before you put in the paneling. If you do not, you will have a

wall that sound will pass through very easily. If the partition is to be tiled for a shower or bathtub, waterproof dry wall must be used or the tile will not hold.

Old walls may be papered with a number of different kinds of wallpaper to cover a multitude of discrepancies and uneven areas that would show through if the wall were simply painted. Dull-finish papers with an active design cover lumpy walls better than high-gloss paper with large designs of continuous color.

Papered walls may be painted over, but the success of the paint job will depend on the condition of the wall and the paper. Dark flat paint will hide imperfections better than a light color. White paint shows every bump and seam.

New structural walls for additions will have to be built on footings extending below the frost line, and foundation walls must conform to the code as in any new construction work.

Floors

Flooring problems: Old floors should be made level and structurally sound before they are refinished and before any remodeling work is done on the house. Sagging floors may indicate weakness in the joists or beams supporting them, and they must be shored up. Sagging could also mean that the footings of a basement column have settled, allowing the floor to sag in the middle. If a floor is high in the center and sags at the outside edge, either the foundation wall is deteriorating or the joists are decaying at the ends where they rest on the wall.

Joists can be strengthened by nailing 2-by-4s to the lower edge and adding additional bridging. Additional joists may be placed across the span. Temporary supports should be used to level the floor first. If the supporting column or its footing needs to be replaced, temporary columns should be placed on either side at the correct height while the column is removed and a new footing poured.

If the exterior foundation wall has deteriorated, causing the floor to sag, or if the joists have decayed on the ends, you will need a professional contractor with a crew experienced in this type of work to arrange support for the entire house until the defective areas are rebuilt.

If there is no bridging between the joists, the addition of bridging alone is often enough to correct the sagging or to firm up a bouncy floor.

A bouncy floor indicates that the joists are not large enough or are spaced too far apart to support the floor adequately and additional support is needed. This can be in the form of a beam at the center of the span, or additional joists plus bridging.

Second floors that sag or bounce are much more of a problem to correct because the trouble is hidden. Sometimes the second floor sags because the attic has been finished off and the original joists were not strong enough to support the added weight of furniture. You will either have to tear up the floor or remove the ceiling to repair it, unless you can shore it up with a steel beam or add a supporting wall on the first floor.

Refinishing: If the floor is level and sound, but the finish is in bad condition, it can be patched and refinished or covered over. Patching and replacing old wood floors that are to be covered with carpet or tile is not difficult. Sanding and refinishing an old wood floor can present many problems, especially if you are living in the house. It does not take as long, nor is it nearly as involved, when the house is empty. Then you do not have to move furniture around or keep the sawdust off your food. Having a floor sanded and refinished is very expensive, although it can be quite handsome when completed. This is a job you can do yourself if you wish. You can rent machines, but you will need a truck or a station wagon and two strong men to help you get the sander in and out. If you plan to do only one room, or one room at a time, expect to have sawdust in and on everything. It will be easier if you can store all the furniture from the rooms you are doing in the garage or in other rooms. With the furniture out of the room, you will be able to do the work more quickly and return the sander to the lumberyard.

First you must do what is called rough sanding. Then you give the floor a second sanding. The heavy machine takes a bit of getting used to, but it can be mastered. It is a good idea to start practicing with it in a bedroom and not in the middle of the living room where mistakes cannot be covered with a bed or another piece of furniture. For a really fine finish, you need to do a third sanding with a disc sander. Then, put on two coats of stain and a *minimum* of two coats of plastic finish (three is recommended) with light sanding by hand between each coat. You will have a beautiful hard finish on the floor that never needs waxing and will last for years. Worn spots in front of doors can easily be repaired with a little hand sanding and touchup.

Floor covering: You may want to use rugs in some areas, perhaps a favorite oriental rug under the coffee table in the living room. It is a waste to refinish floors if you are going to cover them with so-so rugs. There are other flooring materials that are so much easier to work with, such as prefinished parquet wood floor tiles, rubber, vinyl, vinyl asbestos, asphalt, ceramic, and quarry tile. If you want linoleum or some type of cushion vinyl floor covering, it is better to have it installed than to do the installation yourself.

Paint is the quickest, easiest, and least expensive way of covering old floors, and can be surprisingly attractive and durable. A single color painted over the entire floor will make a room seem larger, but if it gets a lot of traffic, the floor will begin to show path marks. A single color has the disadvantage of revealing imperfections, while a floor painted in a pattern will draw your eye to the squares or stripes or whatever pattern you use instead. If paths form on a floor painted in squares or stripes, you can touch up just the worn spots. New paints developed for swimming pools work just as well on wood, and if given two coats of plastic varnish, will wear well.

Heavy wallpaper glued to a smooth wood base and covered with three coats of plastic varnish will give you a glamorous and arresting floor, but will not take the wear that paint will. Try a sample at the door to the room, walk on it every day, and see how well it holds up over a period of time before you do the whole room.

Carpeting: Carpet is unbeatable for warmth, softness, and quiet. Underpadding is essential for longer wear. The carpet market, however, is as confusing and distressing as the inside of a computer which has just blown a fuse. Only a DuPont chemist could possibly understand the different combinations of nylon, acrylic, polyester, orlon, wool, cotton, tufted pile, loop pile, velvet, twist, shag, twist shag, low shag, tweed, combed, and sculptured; or their resistance to staining, wearing, fading, fire, mildew, and static.

Your only answer is a completely reliable store (usually a department store) and a salesman you can trust. Still, it is "buyer beware." Avoid the so-called discount carpet stores that run exciting advertisements in every Sunday paper telling you that for one week only you will get a once-in-a-lifetime buy with prices slashed from $9.88 to $4.99 because they are overstocked and need space in the warehouse for the latest 2,000 miles of carpet they just bought to meet the new season's demand. When you get there, you will find that the selection is limited, they will have just sold the last yard of the carpet they advertised, the color you wanted is not in stock, underpadding is extra, tax is extra, and what they are pushing is a much higher-priced carpet than advertised, though it will be of equally inferior quality. Simply because they claim to be discount houses—"straight from the factory to you"—does not mean they contain any real bargains. Most of the carpet they sell is either left over from motels and big office buildings, or discontinued colors and styles from automobile manufacturers.

Large department stores, while sometimes offering excellent buys on discontinued carpet, usually have people not responsible to the store do the installation. It can be a hit-or-miss proposition and you can end up with an ugly commercial-looking piece of aluminum separating the carpet from the fireplace hearth when what you wanted was a rolled edge that would be inconspicuous.

If you have an old floor with many uneven edges and gaps between the boards, shag carpet over padding will hide just about anything, which is why so many builders use it.

It will also hide pins, cuff links, contact lenses, buttons, and almost anything else you happen to drop on it. All fluffed up, you practically trip over it; all flattened out, it looks wilted. It is difficult to vacuum in either position, and you will need a special beater attachment for the vacuum. Right now, shag carpet is going out of style, so you may find some bargains, if that is the kind of carpet you want.

Before you buy any carpet, get a sample, put a match to it, and see how it burns. If it smolders and exudes toxic fumes, do not buy it. Some carpet, particularly shag carpet with all the air trapped in it, burns very quickly and could spread a small fire all over your house within minutes.

Kitchen carpet is another idea that has seen its day. Anyone who has ever worked in a kitchen and dropped an egg on the floor, stepped on a bit of broccoli or a blueberry, or spilled some flour will tell you to forget it.

Carpet tiles that can be so easily stuck down have the undesirable habit of coming unstuck, especially if you have a playful puppy or cat around. Get a few and test them for at least six months before you buy them.

Vinyl: Cushion vinyl comes in a roll like linoleum and will cover some small cracks and unevenness in the floor, but it could begin to wear unevenly if the variation is pronounced. If a break in the vinyl wearing surface occurs, the entire floor will have to be redone.

Cost alone will not determine the best vinyl. Some of the most expensive will show permanent indentations from chair legs after one dinner. If you can (many salesmen will not want to give you one), get a sample and test it at home. Put it under a chair leg for several days, bend it back and forth, try to burn it, scratch it, cut it, get it dirty, and see how easily it cleans.

Since cushion vinyl comes in sheets, it is difficult to put down yourself, but since it does not have joints or seams, it is easier to keep clean and more sanitary than tile. It is warm, quiet, and soft, and some of the better designs are very good-looking.

Linoleum: An old standby, linoleum is still a good floor covering for the kitchen. The new and improved designs can be used in other rooms as well. It is seamless and easy to keep clean, but should not be considered a "do it yourself" installation since it is almost as hard to put down as cushion vinyl. It will still wear out in front of the sink, as it has been doing for years, but that can be patched. (It will look like a patch, but it can be done.) Not for use below grade, or over concrete.

Inlaid linoleum is more expensive because the colors go all the way through and it does not show wear. It is also tough, greaseproof, and easy to clean. Like linoleum, however, it is affected by dampness and should not be used in the basement or over concrete.

Tile: Asphalt tile is the cheapest tile you can put down easily by yourself. It is not good for the kitchen because it shows stains, is not grease resistant, is brittle and difficult to maintain. But dampness does not affect it and it can be used in the basement and over concrete.

Rubber tile should not be used below grade or over concrete and is a very poor selection for the kitchen or bathroom because it is slippery when wet. It spots easily and needs constant attention, but it wears well and does not show the permanent indentation of chair marks that vinyl asbestos does.

Vinyl asbestos is inexpensive, resistant to grease, and easy to clean, but it shows indentation marks that you can never get out from chairs and high-heeled shoes. The slightest imperfections in the subflooring show through and it is not suitable for kitchens or dining rooms where chair legs dent it and refrigerators on rollers will cut permanent ruts.

Vinyl tile is available in several grades and many styles. It is the most expensive of the man-made tiles, but it wears well, is resistant to almost everything, and is not difficult to care for. It will show indentations, but not as readily as vinyl asbestos, and is no more difficult to put down than the cheapest vinyl asbestos or asphalt.

Ceramic and quarry tile, slate, and brick will cover imperfections in any floor, but they must have a solid and substantial base. Their weight must be taken into consideration, and normal floor joists must be doubled up and reinforced for the additional load of masonry and grout.

If the flooring is in bad shape, none of the various modern tiles should be put on top of it because they will mirror the imperfections underneath and in time will crack and wear thin over such a small thing as a nail head that sticks up a fraction of a millimeter. So if your flooring is in very bad shape, you will either have to remove it or cover it with plywood, hardboard, or some other smooth surface and apply the tile to the new surface (this is easier than removing the old floor).

Ceilings

At one time it was thought that the way to begin remodeling an old house was to have all the ceilings lowered. Many lovely old homes systematically underwent the operation the way most children had their tonsils and adenoids out. In most cases, it was a mistake. Eight-foot-high ceilings are not modern, they are cheap, and that is why we have them. They may save fuel on a gray winter day or at night. But in summer the rooms will be hot and stuffy because there is no space for the warm air to go, and whatever you save on heating will be more than equaled by what you spend on air conditioning to cool the room.

Vary the height: The monotony in so many of today's houses lies in the fact that all ceilings are 8 feet high, level, and white. They do not have to be. If you have a high ceiling, emphasize it, dramatize it, especially if the room is on the south side of the house. Add a floor-to-ceiling window with glass curtains and drapes the entire height.

Even if you only have a one-story tract house, do not consider yourself stuck with ceilings at that boring 8-foot level. Punch a hole right through the ceiling and extend the roof over the ridge, creating a clerestory window for extra height, sunlight in winter, and ventilation in summer.

In other areas, drop the ceiling. If you want to enlarge a room with a window seat on the south facing the street, you can carry the roof

Obviously fake shutters cheapen the look of windows, and the different sizes of glass panes make the picture window (top) awkward and unattractive.

line down quite low over the back of the seat. Line the wall with windows for light and air, but retain privacy by keeping them small and low. The lowness of the ceiling at the windows will make the 8-foot-high areas seem higher. Where you would like more sunlight and there is no problem about privacy, heighten the ceiling with a large shed dormer and run the windows floor to ceiling.

You can drop the ceilings to 7 feet 6 inches in places to change the level—over the fireplace, for example, or over the dining room table, with lights on the dropped section.

Materials: The material most widely used for ceilings is plaster board. It is inexpensive, easy to work with, and can be handled by one man, although on ceiling work it is a good idea to have a helper if you can. Prefinished plywood paneling can be used over the dry wall to save the time, expense, and mess of taping and spackling. The thin plywood will sag if not nailed and glued to the dry wall, and since it is usually glossy, uneven surfaces show up quickly. A dark ceiling will not distribute light well for reading or doing close work, but it can create an interesting space.

Acoustical tile can be glued to the ceiling if the surface is in good condition. Otherwise, you can use furring strips and apply the tile to the strips. If the ceiling is really in bad shape, it is better to remove it.

There are other materials you can use for the ceiling finish besides plaster board, wood paneling, or acoustical tile, but they are in and out of supply, and many are not predictable as to finish, rigidity, durability, and inflammability.

A hung or luminous ceiling will cover pipes and ducts. Acoustical tile panels fit between the suspended frames and lighting panels are interchangeable. Using the same system of hangers and frames, a luminous ceiling can be suspended in the kitchen if there is adequate height. The materials used to install such a ceiling are lightweight and the method is simple. Except for the electricity, anyone can install them.

Windows

Windows do more for a house than just admit light and ventilation. Windows are to a house what eyes are to a person. They can be just as important in adding appearance and character to the facade of the house as our eyes do to our faces—we judge people by their eyes, and people judge our homes by their windows. Poorly proportioned, awkwardly placed windows can ruin an otherwise successfully designed house. When we get older, our eyes do not work as well as they used to, and the same thing can happen to our windows as they age. But happily, we can fix up old windows or buy new ones; and by doing so, change the whole character of the house.

The picture window: Traditional houses do not look good with large expanses of unbroken glass simply because we have inherited our older architectural styles from the Europe of two and three hundred years ago, when glass was made by hand in small panes and joined together with wood or lead to form larger sections. It is these small panes that established the scale and appearance of our Early American and Colonial architectural styles. That is one reason why the picture window, truly an American invention, looks so out of place on houses pretending to be Cape Cod or Colonial. Most picture windows face the street, and that large sheet of glass in the center robs the living room of privacy and wall space. Picture windows are also expensive to curtain, raise the cost of heating, and make the room more difficult to furnish. The worst thing about them, though, is that they are ugly. A picture window should be the first thing to be remodeled when you want to improve the appearance of your home.

The center portion and the side windows can be divided with snap-in dividers to regain some scale and make it more difficult to view the room from the street in the daytime (though you will have to draw the drapes at night). The center, if it is not insulating glass, could be redone into wall. Or the entire window could be removed and replaced with a bay window of better scale and character.

Shutters: If they really work, shutters are fine on windows. But simply nailing them up for show is a waste of money and cheapens the facade because they are such obvious fakes. Having shutters on picture windows, or nailed beside windows that are too big for them, produces the same result. Shutters can sometimes improve the look of a house and add security, but *only* if they really work.

Placement: The placement of windows should be carefully studied from the interior as well as from the exterior of the house. Do not just place a window in the middle of a wall. On the interior, plan the windows around the furniture placement, the view, cross ventilation, and the amount of sun you want in the room. On the exterior, plan them for privacy, balance, security, and ease of cleaning.

Properly placed and sized, windows will cut the cost of heating your home in winter and cooling it in summer. Tall slim windows that open at the bottom and top will let warm air out next to the ceiling and draw cooler air in at the bottom. They also give you more wall space and are easier to drape and shutter for privacy and security.

Styles and types: There is a wide choice in window type, design, and material. Do not make the mistake so many people do of mixing three or four different styles. Double-hung and casement are the only two types of windows that can be combined successfully on traditional architecture, whether it is Early American or Spanish Colonial.

Contemporary houses may use double-hung or casement windows, but they may also use sliding, awning, hopper-style windows in combination with fixed glass. Both contemporary and traditional houses may have a bay, bow,

projected, clerestory, or oriel window, though the design of the sash will be different.

Kinds of Windows

Fixed glass windows (sometimes called "fixed windows") are just what their name implies—windows that do not open. They are inexpensive and, used in combination with other operable windows, cut the cost of a remodeling using a lot of glass. Not only are they cheaper to install, but they also need no screening or weatherstripping.

Double-hung windows offer the best ventilation control. Both top and bottom sash are operable, so cool air can come in at the bottom and warm air go out through the top. Today's version gives you much more control

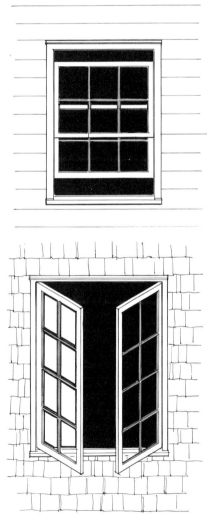

The most common windows: the standard double-hung (top) *and the casement window* (bottom).

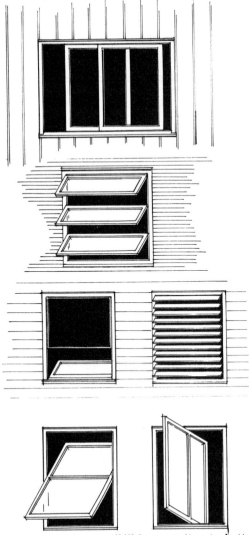

Other fenestration possibilities are: (top to bottom) *sliding, awning, hopper, jalousie* (right), *and pivoted windows.*

Casement windows are the oldest known type and provide 100 percent ventilation, although it is harder to control than the ventilation on a double-hung window. Casement windows open out, and you are supposed to be able to clean them from the inside by reaching your arm through the opening between the open sash and the frame (but some people will find they cannot get their arms through the narrow space). The windows are opened with a crank that is constantly stripping its gear and has to be replaced, so get an extra crank for each new window you buy. Some are available with a metal brace for use in high-wind conditions. Square- or diamond-shaped grills are available and can be very effective.

Sliding windows move back and forth on tracks, which must be kept clean or the windows will stick and bind. The wood windows tend to rattle because of swelling and shrinking. Ventilation is hard to control because the entire height is exposed when the window is open, and only 50 percent of the window may be opened for fresh air.

Awning windows are hinged at the top and swing open at the bottom, offering good ventilation and protection from the rain. Some can be cleaned from the inside, and because of their construction, they need to be washed more often than other windows. Because they must support their own weight when open, they are very heavy, and the horizontal members tend to obscure any view you might have.

Hopper windows are hinged at the bottom and open into the room, which interferes with curtains and drapes. They provide rather poor ventilation and are more associated with motels than houses.

Jalousie windows consist of narrow strips of glass set in a series and opened and closed with a gear or lever. They are most often used in a "Florida" room where maximum ventilation is desired. The angle of the strips prevents rain from entering the house, but it also obscures the view. Jalousies are disturbing when used on traditional homes because of their distinctly modern character.

Pivoted windows are available, but are used more often in industrial buildings than in homes because they cannot be screened and they interfere with drapes when opened. How-

than the traditional counter-balanced windows with old-fashioned weights on ropes that were always wearing out. Now springs make double-hung windows very easy to open. They are fairly easy to clean from the inside, and some may be removed from their frames for cleaning. If made of wood, muntins must be puttied and painted. Newer, and much more preferable, are the vinyl-clad wood windows with snap-in muntins. However, with any double-hung window, you can only get 50 percent of the window open for ventilation.

Single-hung windows are similar to double-hung, but far inferior because only the bottom half can be opened. These should only be used in a garden house or shed.

ever, they can be easily cleaned from the interior and might, in combination with fixed glass, solve a specific problem peculiar to your house.

Bay windows project from the side of the house, with two side windows on an angle and a center one parallel to the house wall. They do not need a separate foundation and can be cantilevered over the foundation. Bay windows are an excellent way to add space to a room and provide more light and ventilation. All three windows may be operable, but only the two side windows need be if you are working on a tight budget.

Bow windows take the form of an unbroken curve that projects from the wall of the house. They can be very appealing, although they are much more expensive than bay windows. Bow windows were originally used by shopkeepers to display their goods and do not open for ventilation. Some modern adaptations with a few operable sashes have been tried in the shape of a bow window, but these are very unattractive.

Projected windows may be of two general types and are simply square bays, the sides rather narrow and with or without glass. They are less expensive than bay windows because they are square. They may also be cantilevered over the foundation to provide a window seat or additional floor space. When they are on the north side of the house, glass in the two sides allows east and west light into the room.

Clerestory windows are high windows usually placed between two intersecting roof planes. They are excellent for providing light to a dark hallway or an interior room. If designed in conjunction with other ventilation, they can circulate air currents to cool the house in summer and warm it in winter. Although high in the wall, they can be controlled from floor level with a worm gear.

Transoms are windows, either operable or fixed, over doors and windows. They allow additional light and air to enter the room and ventilate the warm air next to the ceiling. If, for security reasons, windows and doors are shuttered, transoms still let in light and air.

Remodeling, stripping, reglazing, and repainting old windows is a chore, and you may be ahead in both time and money if you buy new windows instead. Sizes have all changed,

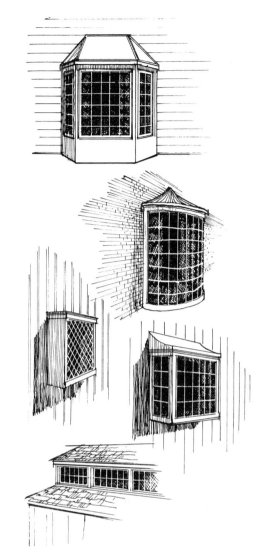

More windows: (top to bottom) *bay, bow, two projected, and a clerestory window.*

and you will have to shop around for windows that come close to the existing openings. Get the correct width, or a narrower one, because the height is easier to change than the width. Although studs are set 16 inches on center, I know of no manufacturer who makes a window to fit this standard module.

Materials: You can buy new windows made of wood, metal, or wood with a vinyl-clad exterior. Wood windows require a lot of maintenance—painting and reputtying—but new ones are fairly inexpensive and come in a wide variety of sizes. Grill inserts that snap out for cleaning and painting can make their care a lot easier.

Window Materials:

Vinyl-clad wood windows are more expensive to buy than simple wood windows, but the installation cost is the same and they are supposed to never need painting. However, "never" is a long time and this type of window has not been around long enough for us to tell much about its durability. It is a good-looking window, with vinyl snap-in muntins, and the saving on time and paint over the years may be worth the extra money.

Aluminum windows may not need painting, but chemicals in the air can corrode and pit the raw shiny metal, so they should be painted for appearance' sake. The inexpensive sliding windows rattle in the slightest breeze, do not fit tightly, and transmit cold through the metal. The type and cost varies from the cheapest to the most expensive, convenient, and trouble-free window there is, with a baked-on enamel finish that requires no upkeep.

Steel windows are more applicable to industrial buildings where fireproofing is a requirement, but they do have their uses in remodeling work. Steel requires painting unless it has a baked-on finish. The advantage of all the metal windows is that they are more stable, are not given to swelling and shrinking, and because of their strength, metal muntins and mullions can be smaller and sashes can carry larger pieces of glass.

Screening: Window screens come in a number of different materials and sizes, which are specified by the number of spaces per inch. For example, a 16-18 screen has sixteen spaces per inch horizontally and eighteen vertically. Tighter mesh will keep out small insects.

Doors

The standard height of a door is 6 feet 8 inches, standard widths vary from 1 foot 6 inches to 3 feet. Interior or exterior grade should be specified when you are ordering. You can buy a door preset in its frame, which makes installation easier, though such a door cannot always be used in remodeling work. Some doors can be ordered in metal or vinyl-clad designs, although these tend to have an embalmed look which is distressing.

Entrance doors: Interior/exterior doors can be single or double, are always hinged, and swing *into* the house. They can be the standard six-panel Colonial type (additional panels are available at extra cost), or they can have glass in one or more panels. There is also the solid-core flush door, which is a single slab of various wood sections covered with exterior-grade plywood. Louvered screened doors are very handsome and provide security, privacy, and fresh air.

Types of Entrance Doors:

Dutch doors are divided horizontally in the middle so the top can open independently of the bottom. They are effective in design, but expensive to weatherstrip and screen properly.

French doors, either single or double, are used for porches and terraces, and are glazed in panes or in one single sheet of glass.

Sliding glass doors of either aluminum, wood, or vinyl are used to open onto porches and terraces and should be glazed only with tempered glass for safety. Muntins of wood or vinyl can snap in and out for better scale and easier cleaning.

Door possibilities: (left to right) *flush, six panel colonial, louvered, decorative light, Dutch, double, single French, double French, and sliding glass door.*

12
Exterior Renovation

One of the biggest mistakes most builders (and many homeowners) make is to use too many different materials on the exterior of a house. The smaller and more modest your house is, the more important it is to simplify the exterior. The inconsistent mixing of vertical siding, stone, brick, and shingles will make the house look smaller, and a bit vulgar.

Never use more than two materials on the facade, and do not stop one material abruptly at a corner and continue around on the other side with a different siding. This is especially true of brick or stone veneer, which if not properly integrated in the design, will look thin and cheap. Changing materials halfway up the middle of a wall is almost always a mistake both from a design standpoint, and from a structural one because, unless correctly flashed, the joint can leak, damaging the interior of the wall.

If you are planning an addition to your house, use the same material on the addition that the house is built of, unless the old walls need to be redone and the whole house can be re-sided in the same material. New siding can completely change the character of a house, so if you are going to re-side, you can accomplish several other things at the same time. You can add insulation to the walls, change and improve the facade, and eliminate future maintenance problems and expense, depending on the siding you choose.

Siding

A new layer of siding on top of the existing walls will provide some insulation in itself, but not enough to equal the regular insulation. The R-value of the insulation rather than its thickness should be checked. The existing walls should be covered with building paper or foil insulating sheets as the new siding is applied.

Clapboard: Probably the most common wood siding, clapboard, is so named because when the early settlers built their new homes of half-timber (which was all right in the gentler climate of Europe) they found it unsuitable in the raw New England winds, and to close the joints in the half-timber, they hastily clapped some boards over the outside walls. The name stuck, though the material is sometimes called beveled siding because now each board is beveled. With the exception of Spanish and Mediterranean, clapboard can be used on all styles of architecture. The scale of the house may be changed by the size of the clapboard used, the amount of face exposed, and the depth of the shadow line determined by the thickness of the board. Deep shadow lines and wide exposure will make the wall seem smaller and more modern. Delicate shadow lines with less face exposed on the narrower clapboards will make the house look larger and more traditional.

Other Siding Materials:

Drop siding is a little more expensive than clapboard because it is milled with a groove at the top and bottom so the boards can be fitted together for better weather protection.

Rabbeted bevel siding is a combination of clapboard and drop siding that provides tighter weather protection than clapboard and a deeper shadow line than drop siding.

Vertical-board siding of uniform- or random-width boards does not provide the weather protection the other sidings do because the boards may shrink and warp, exposing the interior of the wall to moisture. Nailers must be placed on vertical studs to fasten the boards to the wall.

Board and batten siding is similar to vertical-board siding except that it has been made weathertight by the battens, which are nailed over the joints of the boards. Nailers must be provided for conventional vertical studs, but this can be handsome and practical siding that emphasizes the height of the structure.

Wood shingles are about the easiest wood siding you can apply to a house. There is very little waste in cutting, you need no special equipment, and red cedar shingles do not need paint or staining. In a location where there is a lot of rain, wind, and sun, shingles will have to be replaced about every ten to twelve years on the most exposed sides of the house.

Wood shakes are the same as shingles, except they are thicker and of a rougher texture. Shakes last longer than shingles, and hand-split shakes are heavier than the rougher-textured ones.

Aluminum siding with built-in insulation comes with a baked-on finish. The finish may be scraped off and the raw aluminum exposed. Aluminum will dent, sometimes from hail or the careless use of a ladder. Aluminum and other metal-based siding must be grounded to protect your house from falling wires and during electric storms.

Plywood siding can be used as siding if it is exterior grade, but it must be painted or stained.

Texture III is a plywood siding that has grooves in it every 4, 6, or 8 inches, depending on the manufacturer. It is very effective and inexpensive. It goes up very quickly, and can be used on modern or traditional houses. Horizontal joints must be flashed with a metal strip furnished for that purpose and, since vertical joints are subject to leaking, extra felt should be placed behind each joint.

Asphalt shingles have the advantage of being cheap, but rarely look well on walls.

Asbestos shingles are fireproof, come in colors, and never need paint, but their appearance leaves a lot to be desired, especially those designs that attempt to imitate wood. They are not easy to work with and a cutter should be rented to fit them around windows.

There are new hardboards and composition combinations that reproduce the look of brick, stone, and stucco to a remarkable degree, but their effectiveness depends on the design of the facade and the workmanship that goes into installing them. They may not be available in your area.

Paint

Paint, the single best way to improve the exterior appearance of your house, can eliminate ungainly features, emphasize specific lines and detail, soften hard edges, and add weight and dignity to the facade. Paint or stain can also bring together any new additions you add to the house and make them look as if they belonged.

Once you paint anything, it will have to be repainted in the future. Stain has the advantage of protecting the wood as it ages and weathers and does not have to be renewed as often as paint. Cedar shingles or shakes never have to be painted or stained; they can be left to weather naturally. However, painting or staining will increase their weathering capabilities so that they last twice as long.

Using color: The color you paint your house is strictly a personal matter, unless there is a deed restriction saying that all the houses in your area must be painted white or may not be painted some other color. White paint is always acceptable, though it does not hide imperfections as well as color because of the sharp shadows from the sun. Darker grays and earth colors such as soft browns, golds and greens blend repairs and imperfections so that they are much less noticeable.

Window muntins and sashes painted in white or light colors will help screen the interior from the street during the day. Only trim paint should be used on windows because house paint will chalk and the chalking will spread over the glass in a film that will make the windows seem streaked and dirty. Muntins painted a dark color remove the contrast between the dark glass and the dark interior of the room and permit people on the street a better view of the inside of the house.

Small houses can be made to look larger if only one color is used on them, or if one color is used on the walls and another, lighter color on the windows and trim. If you want to use white paint, but are weary of white houses with red, green, blue, or black shutters, paint the shutters white, too. The shadows and different textures will highlight them enough. Avoid the temptation to use primary colors for either walls or trim. These colors may attract attention, but they will cheapen the overall facade (the exception is old-fashioned barn red with white and black trim, which is perfect for some houses).

An awkward or unattractive window can be made to almost disappear if you put louvered shutters on it, leave them closed, and paint them the same color as the wall. If the window is needed to light a dark entrance hall or stair, you can adjust the louvers to permit some light to come through. You could also build a grill over the window, especially if it is

beside the front door and you want to see who is ringing the bell before you answer. Wood slats may be used, or an aluminum radiator grill set in a wood frame and painted to match the wall.

Different styles of windows on a house can give a disconcerting appearance to the facade. This is particularly true if they are placed at random. One solution is to paint all the walls, windows, and trim the same color, saving the entrance door for the one bright spot. This will unify the facade and draw attention to the door and away from the discrepancies in the windows.

If there is a particular window you would like to emphasize, paint everything except it and the front door the same color. Remove shutters that are obvious fakes. This will improve the appearance of your house and also make it seem larger.

A bathroom window next to the front door is very poor placement, especially if it is a large window. You can solve the bathroom window problem in two ways. Shutter the window and paint everything except the door the same color. Or, give the facade of your house a character a bit different from that of your neighbors by using a different material on the entrance, and decreasing the apparent size of the window by leaving only half of it open.

Shingles should not be feathered at the corners. The simple addition of corner boards and the removal of the offending shutters can create quite a different appearance in a small house. Color can transform an ordinary looking house into an unusually good-looking one.

The best paints and stains are expensive, but bargain paint costs even more, because it will necessitate twice as many coats and the surface will have to be repainted sooner. Cheap paint tends to have more faults in it than better paint (but even good paint can fail due to a number of reasons).

Applying paint: The surface to be painted must be properly prepared, or the best and most expensive paints will fail. Concrete, for instance, should be allowed to cure for six months before it is painted because the lime it contains is harmful to paint. Knots in wood

To remodel the exterior of the small development house (top) *with paint, the upper drawing shows wide boards at the corners and on each side of the entrance. The fake shutters are done away with, and operable louvered windows are installed on the large bathroom window near the front door. On the lower scheme, the entrance is further emphasized by using a contrasting material around the door and under the window.*

trim that have not been primed will bleed and show through several coats of paint.

If you paint over an older coat of paint, you must use paint that is compatible with the first or the new coat will "alligator" or separate. This defect is also caused by too much oil thinner, painting over a greasy surface, or painting over an undercoat before it is dry enough. (A less severe defect is called checking.)

Other Problems with Paint:

Blisters form when there is dampness in the wall behind the paint and the paint prevents the moisture from escaping.

Chalking after a time is permissible in moderation because it prevents the buildup of many coats of paint and freshens the color. Paint that chalks excessively should not be used over masonry because the chalking will stain the bricks.

Cracking of paint indicates the use of an inferior paint or preparation, or a lack of sufficient oil in the paint when it was mixed. The cracks will go down to the bare wood, and must be completely removed before repainting.

Crawling is about the worst thing that can happen to paint because it is the hardest defect to correct. The paint forms in globules and you have to wait for it to dry before sanding it down to the first undercoat in good condition. The undercoat then has to be rubbed with steel wool and turpentine before you repaint. Crawling is usually caused by mixing different brands of paint together or painting one glossy coat over another.

Buying paint: There are basically three types of paint and they take their names from the base used in their manufacture: oil, alkyd, and latex. Which one you use depends on what kind of surface you are painting and on the location of your house. If you are in doubt as to which is the best, consult your painter; if you are going to do the work yourself, get the best advice you can from the local paint dealer or lumberyard.

Types of Paint:

Oil-base paint has been with us for centuries, and was at one time the only choice for exterior painting. Now oil-based paint is broken down into three kinds. Pure white-lead paint is the most expensive, holds color the best, and chalks very little. However, in industrial areas it can darken quickly, and since it does not chalk, will look dirty sooner than a titanium-zinc paint, which will not turn dark (it is sometimes called fume-resistant paint). For good color retention, use titanium-dioxide oil-base paint, which is also chalk-resistant. Oil-base paints dry slowly, taking from forty-eight to seventy-two hours, which can be a great disadvantage in bad weather and when scaffolding must be put up. Oil-base paints are thinned with turpentine, which must also be used to clean brushes, rollers, and your hands. If you are doing the work yourself, you will find that cleanup after each painting session is the worst part of the job.

Alkyd paint is made from a synthetic resin and will last from six to eight years. It can be used on wood or masonry for a tough, quick-drying finish in about twenty-four hours. But it must be thinned and cleaned up with mineral spirits or naphtha, which is just as big a bore as turpentine.

Latex and vinyl-plastic paints are marketed under various confusing trade names, and it is important to buy only a well-known brand name. They are expensive, but they are easy to apply, will not blister or chalk, can be put on in damp weather, will dry in an hour, and may be cleaned up with soap and water—all great advantages if you are going to do the work yourself and only have a few free hours a day. Usually one coat will cover, although if it is to be applied on top of another type of paint, the surface may have to be prepared first. New wood and metals have to be sealed before the first coat is applied. The colors hold well and industrial fumes will not darken them. Mildewcides may be added to prevent mildew. Repainting is required in eight to ten years.

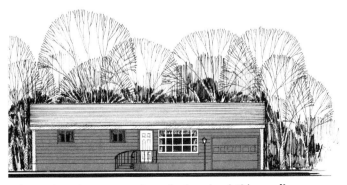

Distracting elements confuse the facade of this small development home (top). The upper scheme uses one paint color for everything except the fascia and corner boards, and a contrasting color to focus attention on the entrance. To highlight a favorite window, paint it, as in the lower scheme, the same color as the entrance, keeping all the other elements subdued.

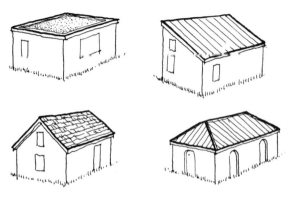
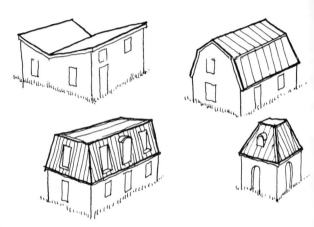

Roof styles: (left to right, top) *flat, shed, butterfly, gambrel.* (bottom) *gable, hip, Mansard, and French roof.*

Roofs

Adding a room or making an addition to a house requires a roof, and the right roof can make or break the remodeling. It is usually better to roof the addition with the same type of roof, using the same pitch, that is on the original part of the house. There are six basic types of roofs: flat, shed, gable, hip, gambrel, and Mansard. Several kinds are compatible with each other. Some are traditionally combined. For instance, in the salt-box design of Early American architecture, a two-story gable-roofed house will have a shed-roofed addition at the back.

Roofing Materials:

Asphalt shingles are the most widely used roofing material and can be applied over a dry existing roof without removing the old shingles. The roof pitch required is a minimum of 3 inches to the foot. The minimum weight accepted by the FHA is the 235-pound shingle— the number of shingles weighing a total of 235 pounds required to cover 100 square feet. But 300-pound shingles weather better and should be used if possible.

Asphalt shingles are not fireproof, but if the mineral granules on the surface are in good condition, they may briefly retard a fire caused by falling embers from a nearby fire. None of the colors are good, so choose neutral gray, black, or white.

Built-up asphalt or hot-pitch roofs are used on flat roofs. Hot asphalt is alternated with layers of felt and topped with gravel. The roof is guaranteed for from ten to twenty years, depending on the number of plys of felt and tar.

Wood shingles cost more than asphalt. They are a standby for traditional American styles of architecture, and just as adaptable for modern and contemporary homes. They last ten to twenty years and their durability is increased by soaking them in a preservative stain. They do burn readily so some codes prohibit their use in certain areas.

Wood shakes are thick shingles and are more expensive. Hand-split shakes have a rough, sturdy texture. If you have them on the wall, do not use shakes or shingles on the roof without changing the color or texture.

Asbestos shingles are fireproof and must be used on a minimum pitch of 5 inches to the foot. Although they are heavy and weigh 250 to 600 pounds per square (100 square feet), they are brittle and should not be walked on.

Slate and clay tile have a minimum pitch to which they can be applied, depending on the design. Their own weight prohibits them from being used on structures unless they have been designed for them.

Aluminum shingles are fireproof, but usually are used only on commercial buildings. Their main disadvantage is the baked-on finish, which is shiny and produces a poor imitation of shakes.

Corrugated metal, of either steel or aluminum, can be used in remodeling, but only if the entire roof is reroofed—and it takes a pretty competent designer to handle the aesthetics. Steel requires painting or it will rust, and because of its shiny surface, you may want to paint the aluminum. These are fireproof, of course, can be used with corrugated plastic as skylights, and require a minimum pitch of 3 inches to the foot.

Glossary

Alligatoring   An advanced form of cracking and checking on the surface of paint where it has pulled away from the wood.

Anchor bolt   A heavy bolt imbedded in masonry to secure a wooden sill to the foundation.

Angle iron   A strip of metal in the form of an L, used to support masonry over openings.

Apron   A finished piece of wood below the sill of a window used to cover the rough edge.

Ash dump   A metal frame with a metal door placed in the floor of a fireplace through which ashes are disposed of by being dumped into the ash pit at the base of the chimney.

Asphalt   A mineral pitch or tar used on built-up roofs and the exterior foundation walls of basements to waterproof them.

Asphalt shingles   Shingles combining asphalt pitch and coated with mineral granules.

Atrium   A large, completely enclosed garden open to the sky, with the principal rooms of the house arranged around it.

Awning door   A door whose central position is fitted with an awning window.

Awning window   A pane of glass or a series of panes set in a frame and opening outward from the bottom.

Back filling   Soil and broken stones used to level around the foundation walls and provide a slope for water to be drained away from the house.

Balustrade   A railing made up of posts connected at the top by a handrail.

Base shoe   A strip of molding nailed to the baseboard next to the floor.

Battens   Thin narrow strips of wood used to cover joints in vertical wood siding.

Batts   Insulating material composed of mineral fiber with a vapor barrier on one side, sized to fit between stud walls, joists, and rafters.

Beam   A large piece of timber or metal used to support floor and ceiling joists.

Bearing plate   A metal plate placed under a column or beam to distribute the weight of the load.

Bearing wall   A wall that carries the load from floor joists and partitions above it.

Blistering   A defect in which paint film pulls away from the surface painted.

Board foot   A unit of measure for lumber. One board foot would be a piece of lumber 1 foot square and approximately 1 inch thick.

Bond   The pattern in which brickwork is done.

Bow window   Glass panes set in a frame on a continuous curve.

Box out   A term meaning to cover columns, beams, pipes, or wiring with another material to improve their appearance.

Branch pipe   A special plumbing pipe with one or more branches.

Brick veneer   A layer of brick, one brick thick, attached to the surface of a wall, but carrying no load except its own weight.

Bridging   Pieces of wood or metal straps crisscrossed between joists to stiffen them and hold them in place.

Building line   The limit to which you are permitted to build or extend your house in relation to the edge of your property.

Built-up beam   A beam formed by nailing or bolting two or more planks together to increase their strength.

Built-up roof   A roofing material used on flat roofs consisting of a number of plys of roofing felt and hot pitch topped with gravel.

Cantilever   A structural overhang projecting beyond the supporting wall or column.

Cased opening   A finished opening with trim, but no door.

Casement   A window hinged on its vertical edge.

Casing   Framework around a window or door.

Chalking   The powdering of the top surface of paint.

Cinder block Building block made of cement and cinders. Used because it is light in weight.

Clapboard Long boards, thin on top and thicker on bottom, used horizontally for siding.

Clerestory A wall containing windows raised above surrounding roofs.

Collar beam A horizontal tie beam connecting, and parallel to, two opposite rafters.

Condensation Warm, moist air changing to drops of water on a cold surface, such as glass or metal.

Convection Transmission of heat by the natural motion of air or water after it has come in contact with the heat source.

Coping The top course of a masonry wall.

Corner boards Vertical boards used to trim the corner of an exterior frame wall.

Cornice The decorative construction at the intersection of the roof and side wall at the eaves.

Corrosion The rusting or oxidation of two different metals by contact and interaction with oxygen in a damp atmosphere.

Crawl space The unexcavated space enclosed by the foundation walls under the first floor of a house.

Dead load Weight of structure and finishing materials carried by joist and structural walls and beams.

Delaminate Separation of plywood plys due to moisture.

Dormer window A vertical window in a sloping roof.

Double-hung window A window with upper and lower vertical sliding sashes.

Down light An incandescent light fixture recessed into the ceiling so that only the floor or furniture under the fixture is lighted.

Dress To smooth and finish wood or masonry.

Dressed-size lumber A term referring to the actual size of lumber. For instance, a 2-by-4 stud is really $1\frac{5}{8}$ inches by $3\frac{5}{8}$ inches.

Dry stone wall A masonry wall laid without mortar.

Dry wall This term refers to any interior wall finish that does not use plaster. However, it usually means $\frac{3}{8}$-inch or $\frac{1}{2}$-inch gypsum wallboard or Sheetrock with the joints taped and spackled.

Ducts Large rectangular or round tubes used to distribute air from the furnace or air-conditioning unit to registers in the rooms. They may be constructed of plastic, metal, asbestos, or composition materials.

Dutch door A door divided horizontally so the top half may be opened while the lower section remains closed.

Easement An acquired right to use part of the land belonging to someone else.

Eaves The part of the roof that projects over the side walls.

Efflorescence White powder that forms on the surface of brick and masonry.

Escutcheon A metal plate or shield placed around and behind the doorknob and keyhole to protect the wood of the door.

Eyebrow dormer A low window in a roof over which the roof is carried in a wavy line similar to an arch.

Facade The exterior appearance of a house or elevation.

Fascia The flat horizontal board at the outer face of the cornice.

Fenestration The arrangement and design of doors and windows in a wall.

Finished floor Hardwood, tile, or carpet laid over the subfloor.

Finished hardware Doorknobs, locks, hinges, and any exposed hardware in a house.

Fire stops The blocking of air passages to prevent the spread of fire within the wall.

Flashing Sheet metal used at all intersections of walls and roofs, at changes in materials, and over doors and windows to prevent the leakage of water into the house.

Floating Bringing a smooth finish to cement or concrete.

Footing The foundation for a column or a wall which distributes the weight carried by the column or wall over a greater area. Footings are usually concrete and are placed below the frost line to prevent structural damage from freezing.

Forms Enclosures made with wood or metal to shape and hold the wet ("green") concrete until it has set and dried sufficiently to support itself and imposed loads.

Frame construction The type of building

which is made of lumber using wood studs, joists, and beams.

Framing The process of putting together the studs, joists, beams, plates, flooring, roofing, and partitions to build a house.

French door One or a pair of doors with glazed panels extending the full length of the door.

Furring The act of applying furring strips to provide an air space between structural walls and the interior finish or to level an uneven surface.

Furring strips Narrow strips of wood or metal.

Gable The triangular portion of an end wall contained between the sloping eaves of a ridge roof.

Gable roof A ridged roof ending at one or both ends in a gable.

Galvanizing The application of a zinc coat to iron or steel to prevent rusting.

Gambrel roof A ridge roof with a double slope, the lower slope being the steeper of the two.

Garret window A skylight with the glass incorporated into the slope of the roof.

Gazebo A summer house in a garden.

Glaze The installation of glass in windows and doors.

Glazed tile Masonry tile with a hard glossy surface.

Grading Filling in around the building with earth so water will drain away from the foundations. It may also mean the smoothing and proper leveling of a driveway.

Grout A cement mixture used to fill crevices.

Half-story The attic in a pitched roof with sloping walls, having some flat ceiling and a floor.

Hardpan A compacted layer of earth and clay which is very difficult to excavate.

Hardwood It does not refer to the actual hardness of the wood, but to a botanical group of trees, such as maple, oak, and other broad-leafed trees.

Hip roof A ridge roof in which the gables have been replaced by sloping sections of roof.

Hopper window A window sash with hinges at the bottom and opening into the room.

Hydrostatic head Water pressure from a high-water table on the underside of the basement floors and walls that forces moisture and water into the basement.

I-beam A steel beam in the shape of a capital I; used many times in remodeling to support walls and floors when the structural partitions and bearing walls have been removed.

Indirect lighting A system of lighting the walls and ceiling of a room with fixtures that cannot be seen.

Inglenook A Scandinavian word meaning built-in seating close to and around the fireplace.

Jalousie window Unframed strips of glass set in a series that opens from the bottom to prevent rain from coming in the house.

Jamb The vertical side posts used in framing a door or window.

Joist One of a number of timbers used to support floors and ceilings. Joists are used in series set edgewise, and are in turn supported by bearing walls, structural partitions, or beams.

Kiln-dried A term used to refer to lumber that has been dried in a kiln with controlled heat and humidity to artificially season it.

Knee wall A low wall in the attic running parallel to the ridge that closes off the unusable triangular section next to the floor.

Lally column A round steel pipe, usually 4 inches in diameter and sometimes filled with concrete, used to support beams.

Laminate To build up layers of wood or other material held together with glue. Plywood is a good example of lamination.

Lath Small strips of wood about ⅜ inch thick and 1 inch wide, used to support plaster, seal cracks between boards, and build decorative screens. Wood lath for use with plaster has been replaced by metal lath in the few areas in which plaster is still used.

Leader A pipe or down spout that carries rainwater from the gutter to the ground.

Lean-to A small addition having a shed roof

which is supported by the wall of the house.

Lien   A legal claim against the owner of a house by a contractor who has not been paid for work and materials supplied.

Light   A single windowpane.

Lineal foot   A line 1 foot long, as distinguished from a square foot or a cubic foot.

Lintel   A steel, wood, or stone beam placed horizontally over an opening in a wall to support the wall above it.

Live load   Weight of furniture and occupants on joist and structural walls and beams.

Loft   A room or platform directly under the roof.

Loggia   An arcade with a roof and one open side.

Louver   An opening for ventilation containing slanted members to keep out rain.

Mansard roof   A type of roof named after the French architect who developed it in Paris during the Renaissance to conform to the height restrictions, while actually adding an extra story to a building. It has two slopes, the lower one very steep and almost vertical, the upper one almost flat.

Mastic   A thick adhesive used for bedding glass, setting tile, and repairing roofs.

Metal ties   Steel straps coated with Portland cement and used to tie brick or stone veneer to a frame wall.

Modular design and construction   Using a module of 4 feet so residential work is more economical and there is less waste. Studs and joists are placed on 16-inch centers with a ceiling height of 8 feet, which permits plywood and interior finishes to be used without cutting and waste since they are manufactured in sheets 4 feet by 8 feet.

Module   A unit of measure used by architects and designers.

Mullion   The vertical division between a series of windows. Generally included in the term "muntin."

Muntin   The division between windowpanes both vertical and horizontal.

Nail sizes   The size of a nail is indicated by the word "penny," which was originally the price per hundred. Lengths may vary slightly from standard because of different manufacturers, but in general a 2d (the "d" stands for penny) nail is 1 inch long, the 4d is 1½ inches, the 6d is 2 inches, the 8d is 2½ inches, the 10d is 3 inches, the 20d is 4 inches, and the 60d is 6 inches.

Nailing strips   Pieces of wood to which finish material is nailed; similar to furring strips.

Nonbearing walls   Partitions that do not carry overhead partitions or joists. They support only their own weight and serve to divide space into rooms.

Nosing   The rounded edge of a stair tread.

Oriel window   A window on the upper floors of a house that projects from the wall and is supported by a decorative brace.

Orientation   The location of the house—the direction it faces.

Outlet   Electrical term meaning the place where a fixture, plug, or switch is to be connected.

Overhang   The projection of a floor or roof over an outside wall.

Overloading   Placing too much weight on a beam, column, or a floor.

Palladian window   A tall elegant window with a circular top flanked by two square-topped windows reaching only the tangent of the circle.

Parquet floor   Pieces of wood set in a pattern.

Party wall   A structural wall shared by two houses.

Penny   The term of measurement for nail lengths. See *Nail sizes.*

Perspective drawing   A sketch of a house taken from a particular location.

Pilaster   A column attached to a wall.

Pillar   A supporting masonry shaft made of smaller pieces of marble, stone, or brick. It differs from a column in that a column is one piece of solid material, such as steel.

Pin spots   Incandescent lights recessed into the ceiling for special lighting effects, such as lighting a sculpture or flower arrangement.

Pitch Various combinations of coal tar insoluble in water and used in plumbing and other construction work.

Pitch of a roof The angle of slope on a roof.

Pivoted window A casement window that pivots either horizontally or vertically.

Plank A heavy piece of timber thicker than a board, usually 1½ inches thick and more than 6 inches wide.

Plaster of paris This is the term used for calcined gypsum (large deposits of it were once found near Paris).

Plasterboard Gypsum that is covered on both sides with paper, often called dry wall or gypboard.

Plate A 2-by-4 or larger piece of lumber placed on top of a stud wall or masonry so that joists and rafters may be fastened to it.

Plumb bob A weight attached to a string for testing the trueness of perpendicular surfaces.

Pointing Finishing of joints in a masonry wall.

Portico An open space attached to a house as a porch, or completely detached with a roof supported with columns.

Portland cement Silica, lime, and alumnia mixed together and fired in a kiln. The clinkers are then ground fine to produce a strong hydraulic cement.

Priming The first coat of paint, usually a special primer, put on wood or metal to make a hard opaque surface that will take additional coats of paint well.

Quarry-faced masonry A rough squared stone with the face as it was split in the quarry.

Quarry-tile Machine-made unglazed tile of a reddish-brown color.

Quarter round A molding that is a quarter of a circle.

Rabbet A section cut out of wood and timber to receive another board cut to fit it.

Radiant heating A system of heating that uses the floor, walls, or ceiling as a heating panel, with warmed pipes or wires imbedded in it.

Rafter The sloping member of the roof structure that runs from the plate to the ridge.

Reinforced concrete Concrete that has been given greater strength by steel bars imbedded in it.

Rendering A finished perspective painting of the house in ink, watercolor, or some other medium.

Retaining wall A wall built to hold back the soil.

Return The continuation of a molding in another direction.

Rheostat An electrical device regulating current to light fixtures so the brightness can be controlled.

Ridge The top of the roof where two slopes meet.

Riser The vertical board under the tread of a step.

Rock wool A product manufactured from granite, silica, calcium, and magnesium that looks like wool, but is vermin-, fire-, and damproof and is used as insulation.

Rough floor A subfloor that serves as a base for the finished flooring material.

Rough opening An unfinished opening in which the window and door frames will be placed.

Saddle The ridge covering of a roof. Also a board or marble covering the floor joint in a doorway where the material changes from wood to tile.

Sash The frame for one or more windowpanes.

Sawtooth roof A roof used in factories for admitting light to the interior.

Scale There are two kinds of scale. Architects do drawings to scale, denoting the size of the drawings in relation to the full size house: i.e., ¼ inch = 1 foot means that ¼ inch on the drawings represents 1 foot in the actual house. The architect does this measuring and drawing with an expensive ruler, also called a scale. Architects also speak of scale in relation to appropriateness and proportion of elements in the design of a house. If something is out of scale, it is either too large or too small for the rest of the house (or room).

Section A drawing of the house seen from a given point, as if it were a loaf of bread cut down the middle.

Shake A heavy wood shingle.

Sheathing Plywood or boards nailed to the studs and roof rafters on the exterior of a house as a foundation for the finish siding and roofing.

Shed roof A roof sloping in one direction with a single pitch.

Shim A thin, tapered piece of shingle used in leveling work.

Shingle Thin pieces of wood or other material that is tapered and used to cover walls or roofs.

Shore A piece of timber used as a temporary support.

Side lights Small vertical windows on each side of a door.

Sill The lowest horizontal member of a frame supporting a house, or the lowest member under a door or a window.

Sleepers Strips of wood laid over rough concrete floors so a finished wood floor can be applied over them.

Soffit The underside of overhangs.

Soil pipe A vertical pipe carrying off waste from the toilet.

Span The distance between supports for joist and rafters.

Square A term denoting roofing materials measuring 100 square feet.

Stick built Not prefabricated in any way. Built stud by stud and joist by joist.

Stud A vertical piece of lumber, usually a 2-by-4, used in concert with others to form walls and partitions.

Subfloor The plywood or boards applied directly to the floor joists as part of the rough work. The finished floor is placed on top of the subfloor.

Terrazzo A mixture of marble chips and cement, ground and polished smooth. It is used for floors and can be given a high polish.

Thermostat An electrically controlled device to regulate the heat and air conditioning.

Three-way switch An electric switch that allows a light fixture to be controlled from two separate places.

Tie beam A beam that prevents the spreading apart of rafters.

Toenailing Nailing at an angle to attach one piece of lumber to another.

Top plate The horizontal member nailed to the top of a partition.

Transite Manufactured fireproof sheets made of a combination of asbestos and cement.

Transom A window over a door or over another window.

Trap A vertical bend in the water pipe of each plumbing fixture that stays full of water and prevents offensive odors from entering the house or a room of a house.

Trowel A flat steel tool used to spread and smooth mortar and cement.

Truss A combination of wood or steel members that work together to span distances that none could approach alone.

Valley The intersection of two roofs.

Vapor barrier Material used to keep moisture from penetrating walls.

Variance Written permission from a zoning board to build or remodel in a manner that is acceptable in this one instance only.

Veneered wall Brick or stone that is not bonded together, but attached to a frame wall with clips, and does not carry any load but its own weight.

Wainscot A lining or paneling for the lower part of an interior wall.

Wallboard Gypsum, wood, plastic, and many other materials that are used to finish walls on the interior of a house and around a shower or tub.

Weatherstrip A flange of metal or plastic covering joints to keep out drafts around doors and windows.

Wet wall A term referring to walls that contain soil pipes, hot- and cold-water pipes, and vents.

Winders Treads of stairs shaped like a triangle and used at corners.

Index